studysync®

Reading & Writing Companion

True to Yourself

Who are you meant to be?

studysync

studysync.com

Send all inquiries to:
BookheadEd Learning, LLC
610 Daniel Young Drive
Sonoma, CA 95476

ISBN 978-1-94-469578-1

2 3 4 5 6 7 QVS 23 22 21 20 19

A

Student Guide

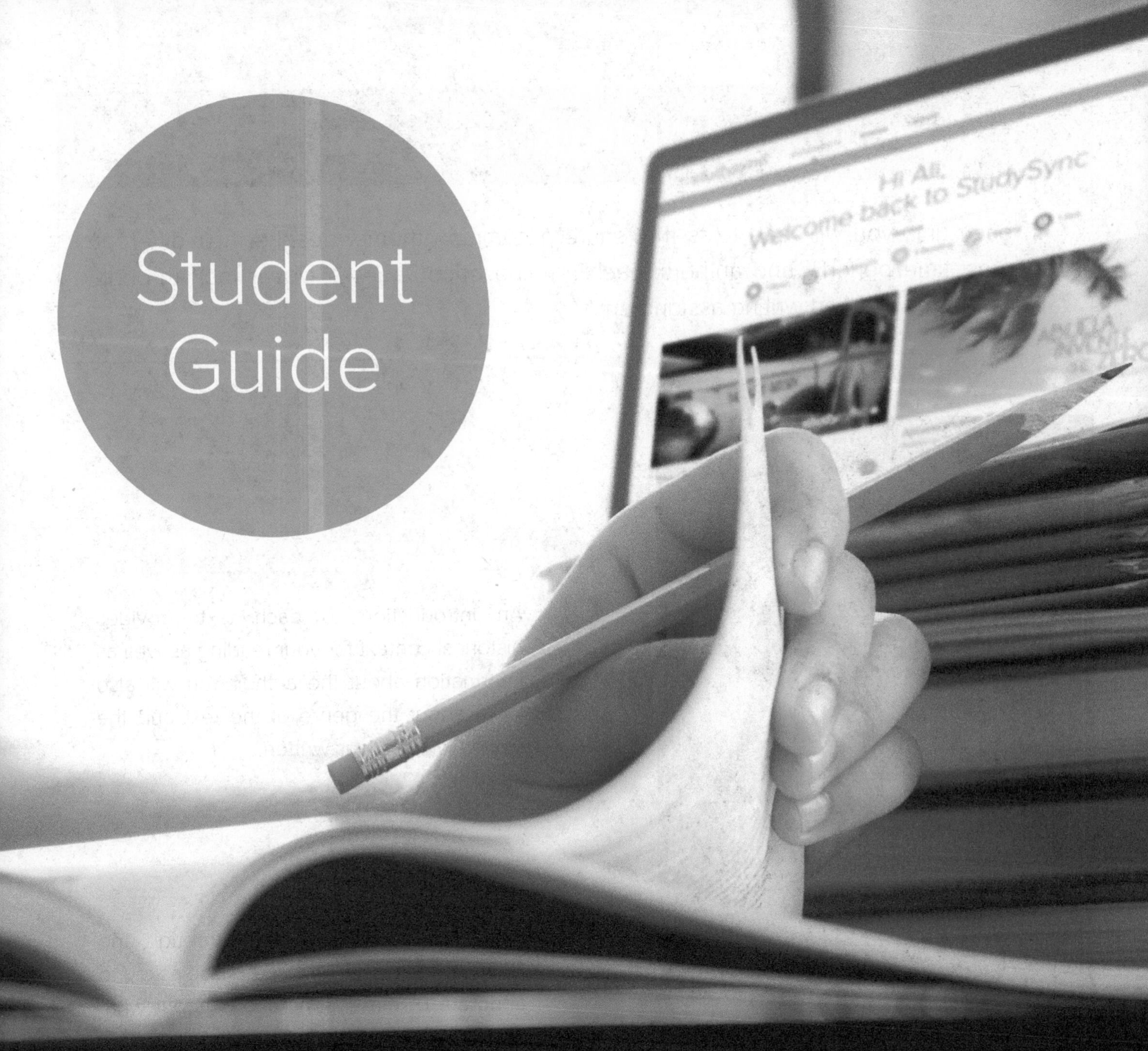

Getting Started

Welcome to the StudySync Reading & Writing Companion! In this book, you will find a collection of readings based on the theme of the unit you are studying. As you work through the readings, you will be asked to answer questions and perform a variety of tasks designed to help you closely analyze and understand each text selection. Read on for an explanation of each section of this book.

Close Reading and Writing Routine

In each unit, you will read texts that share a common theme, despite their different genres, time periods, and authors. Each reading encourages a closer look through questions and a short writing assignment.

1 Introduction studysync

Sandra Cisneros (b. 1954) is a renowned Chicana writer whose poems, novels, and short stories explore the complicated struggle of finding one's own identity. Cisneros is best known for her novel *The House on Mango Street* and the collection *Woman Hollering Creek and Other Stories*. "Eleven" is from the latter, the story of a girl named Rachel who experiences growing pains on her eleventh birthday. When her teacher insists that an ugly red sweater belongs to Rachel, the eleven-year-old has exceptional thoughts but can't share them. Even so, it's evident that the protagonist of Sandra Cisneros's short story has insight beyond her years.

"You open your eyes and everything's just like yesterday, only it's today. And you don't feel eleven at all."

1 What they don't understand about birthdays and what they never tell you is that when you're eleven, you're also ten, and nine, and eight, and seven, and six, and five, and four, and three, and two, and one. And when you wake up on your eleventh birthday you expect to feel eleven, but you don't. You open your eyes and everything's just like yesterday, only it's today. And you don't feel eleven at all. You feel like you're still ten. And you are—underneath the year that makes you eleven.

2 Like some days you might say something stupid, and that's the part of you that's still ten. Or maybe some days you might need to sit on your mama's lap because you're scared, and that's the part of you that's five. And maybe one day when you're all grown up maybe you will need to cry like if you're three, and that's okay. That's what I tell Mama when she's sad and needs to cry. Maybe she's feeling three.

3 Because the way you grow old is kind of like an onion or like the rings inside a tree trunk or like my little wooden dolls that fit one inside the other, each year inside the next one. That's how being eleven years old is.

4 You don't feel eleven. Not right away. It takes a few days, weeks even, sometimes even months before you say Eleven when they ask you. And you don't feel smart eleven, not until you're almost twelve. That's the way it is.

5 Only today I wish I didn't have only eleven years rattling inside me like pennies in a tin Band-Aid box. Today I wish I was one hundred and two instead of eleven because if I was one hundred and two I'd have known what to say when Mrs. Price put the red sweater on my desk. I would've known how to tell her it wasn't mine instead of just sitting there with that look on my face and nothing coming out of my mouth.

6 "Whose is this?" Mrs. Price says, and she holds the red sweater up in the air for all the class to see. "Whose? It's been sitting in the coatroom for a month."

Skill: Figurative Language

The narrator uses similes when she compares aging to everyday things. When I picture onions, tree trunks, and wooden dolls, I notice they all have layers. She must mean that when you get older, you keep getting more layers.

1 Introduction

An Introduction to each text provides historical context for your reading as well as information about the author. You will also learn about the genre of the text and the year in which it was written.

2 Notes

Many times, while working through the activities after each text, you will be asked to **annotate** or **make annotations** about what you are reading. This means that you should highlight or underline words in the text and use the "Notes" column to make comments or jot down any questions you have. You may also want to note any unfamiliar vocabulary words here.

You will also see sample student annotations to go along with the Skill lesson for that text.

3 First Read

During your first reading of each selection, you should just try to get a general idea of the content and message of the reading. Don't worry if there are parts you don't understand or words that are unfamiliar to you. You'll have an opportunity later to dive deeper into the text.

4 Think Questions

These questions will ask you to start thinking critically about the text, asking specific questions about its purpose, and making connections to your prior knowledge and reading experiences. To answer these questions, you should go back to the text and draw upon specific evidence to support your responses. You will also begin to explore some of the more challenging vocabulary words in the selection.

5 Skills

Each Skill includes two parts: Checklist and Your Turn. In the Checklist, you will learn the process for analyzing the text. The model student annotations in the text provide examples of how you might make your own notes following the instructions in the Checklist. In the Your Turn, you will use those same instructions to practice the skill.

Eleven

3

First Read

Read "Eleven." After you read, complete the Think Questions below.

4

THINK QUESTIONS

1. How does Rachel feel about the red sweater that is placed on her desk? Respond with textual evidence from the story as well as ideas that you have inferred from clues in the text.
2. According to Rachel, why does Sylvia say the sweater belongs to Rachel? Support your answer with textual evidence.
3. Write two or three sentences exploring why Mrs. Price responds as she does when Phyllis claims the sweater. Support your answer with textual evidence.
4. Find the word **raggedy** in paragraph 9 of "Eleven." Use context clues in the surrounding sentences, as well as the sentence in which the word appears, to determine the word's meaning. Write your definition here and identify clues that helped you figure out its meaning.
5. Use context clues to determine the meaning of **nonsense** as it is used in paragraph 15 of "Eleven." Write your definition here and identify clues that helped you figure out its meaning. Then check the meaning in a dictionary.

Eleven

5

Skill:
Figurative Language

Use the Checklist to analyze Figurative Language in "Eleven." Refer to the sample student annotations about Figurative Language in the text.

CHECKLIST FOR FIGURATIVE LANGUAGE

To determine the meaning of figures of speech in a text, note the following:

- ✓ words that mean one thing literally and suggest something else
- ✓ similes, such as "strong as an ox"
- ✓ metaphors, such as "her eyes were stars"
- ✓ personification, such as "the daisies danced in the wind"

In order to interpret the meaning of a figure of speech in context, ask the following questions:

- ✓ Does any of the descriptive language in the text compare two seemingly unlike things?
- ✓ Do any descriptions include "like" or "as" that indicate a simile?
- ✓ Is there a direct comparison that suggests a metaphor?
- ✓ Is a human quality is being used to describe this animal, object, force of nature or idea that suggests personification?
- ✓ How does the use of this figure of speech change your understanding of the thing or person being described?

YOUR TURN

5

1. How does the figurative language in paragraph 18 help readers understand Rachel's reaction to the sweater?
   - O A. The metaphors in the paragraph help readers understand how uncomfortable Rachel feels in the sweater.
   - O B. The similes in the paragraph help readers understand how uncomfortable Rachel feels in the sweater.
   - O C. The metaphors in the paragraph make it clear to readers that Rachel is overreacting about the sweater.
   - O D. The similes in the paragraph make it clear to readers that Rachel is overreacting about the sweater.
2. How does the figurative language in paragraph 19 help readers visualize Rachel's behavior?
   - O A. The mention of "little animal noises" tells readers that Rachel is acting more like an animal than a human.
   - O B. The metaphor of "clown-sweater arms" shows that Rachel is able to see the humorous side in her experience.
   - O C. The similes about her body shaking "like when you have the hiccups" and her head hurting "like when you drink milk too fast" connect to unpleasant experiences most readers have had.
   - O D. The statement that "there aren't any more tears left in [her] eyes" suggests that Rachel is starting to calm down.

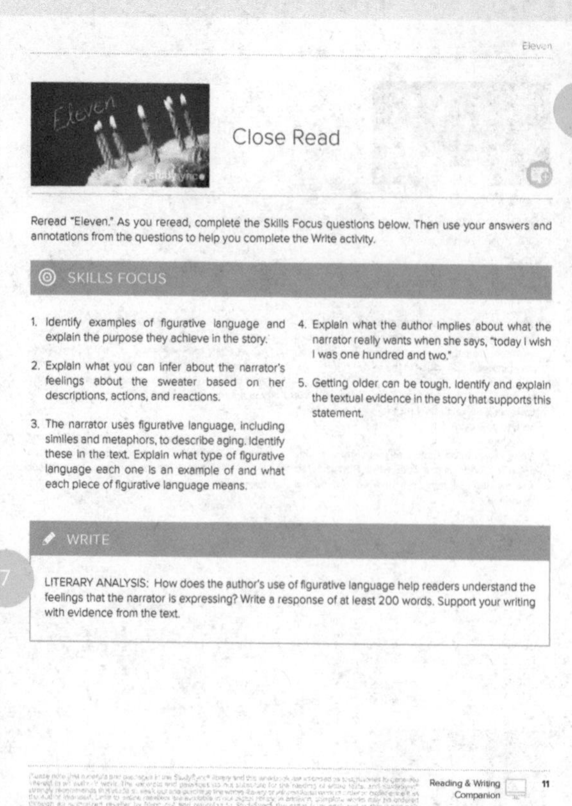
Eleven

Close Read

Reread "Eleven." As you reread, complete the Skills Focus questions below. Then use your answers and annotations from the questions to help you complete the Write activity.

SKILLS FOCUS

1. Identify examples of figurative language and explain the purpose they achieve in the story.
2. Explain what you can infer about the narrator's feelings about the sweater based on her descriptions, actions, and reactions.
3. The narrator uses figurative language, including similes and metaphors, to describe aging. Identify these in the text. Explain what type of figurative language each one is an example of and what each piece of figurative language means.
4. Explain what the author implies about what the narrator really wants when she says, "today I wish I was one hundred and two."
5. Getting older can be tough. Identify and explain the textual evidence in the story that supports this statement.

WRITE

LITERARY ANALYSIS: How does the author's use of figurative language help readers understand the feelings that the narrator is expressing? Write a response of at least 200 words. Support your writing with evidence from the text.

Reading & Writing Companion 11

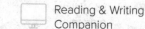

Lost Island

FICTION

Introduction

Marina wakes up alone, thirsty, and hungry on a deserted island. How did she get here, and why is her head throbbing? As she slowly recalls a large wave smashing into Uncle Merlin's fishing boat, Marina takes her first steps towards survival.

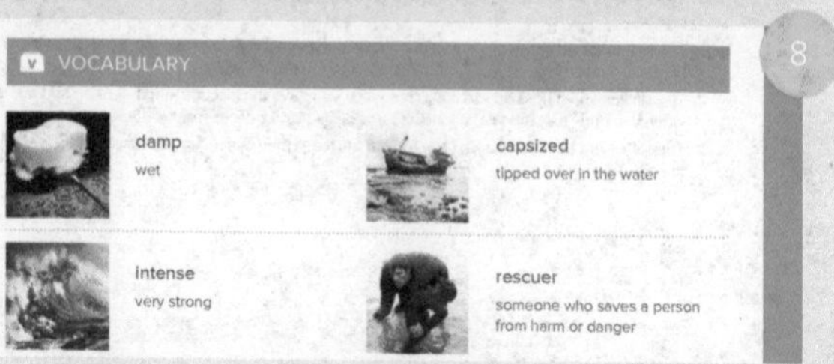
VOCABULARY

damp
wet

capsized
tipped over in the water

intense
very strong

rescuer
someone who saves a person from harm or danger

6 Close Read & Skills Focus

After you have completed the First Read, you will be asked to go back and read the text more closely and critically. Before you begin your Close Read, you should read through the Skills Focus to get an idea of the concepts you will want to focus on during your second reading. You should work through the Skills Focus by making annotations, highlighting important concepts, and writing notes or questions in the "Notes" column. Depending on instructions from your teacher, you may need to respond online or use a separate piece of paper to start expanding on your thoughts and ideas.

7 Write

Your study of each selection will end with a writing assignment. For this assignment, you should use your notes, annotations, personal ideas, and answers to both the Think and Skills Focus. Be sure to read the prompt carefully and address each part of it in your writing.

8 English Language Learner

The English Language Learner texts focus on improving language proficiency. You will practice learning strategies and skills in individual and group activities to become better readers, writers, and speakers.

Extended Writing Project

This is your opportunity to use genre characteristics and craft to compose meaningful, longer written works exploring the theme of each unit. You will draw information from your readings, research, and own life experiences to complete the assignment.

1 Writing Project

After you have read all of the unit text selections, you will move on to a writing project. Each project will guide you through the process of writing your essay. Student models will provide guidance and help you organize your thoughts. One unit ends with an **Extended Oral Project** which will give you an opportunity to develop your oral language and communication skills.

2 Writing Process Steps

There are four steps in the writing process: Plan, Draft, Revise, and Edit and Publish. During each step, you will form and shape your writing project, and each lesson's peer review will give you the chance to receive feedback from your peers and teacher.

3 Writing Skills

Each Skill lesson focuses on a specific strategy or technique that you will use during your writing project. Each lesson presents a process for applying the skill to your own work and gives you the opportunity to practice it to improve your writing.

True to Yourself

Who are you meant to be?

Genre Focus: **REALISTIC FICTION**

Texts

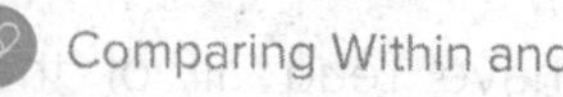

1 Bronx Masquerade
REALISTIC FICTION *Nikki Grimes*

9 A BEACON of Hope: The Story of Hannah Herbst
INFORMATIONAL TEXT *Rebecca Harrington*

12 Shree Bose: Never Too Young to Save the World
INFORMATIONAL TEXT *Amanda Sperber*

27 Letter to His Daughter
INFORMATIONAL TEXT *W.E.B. Du Bois*

36 The Story Behind the Bus
INFORMATIONAL TEXT *The Henry Ford Museum*

40 Rosa
POEM *Rita Dove*

42 Rosa Parks: My Story
INFORMATIONAL TEXT *Rosa Parks*

54 Eleanor Roosevelt: A Life of Discovery
INFORMATIONAL TEXT *Russell Freedman*

58 Brave
REALISTIC FICTION *Svetlana Chmakova*

77 I Never Had It Made: An Autobiography of Jackie Robinson
INFORMATIONAL TEXT *Jackie Robinson*

87 Touching Spirit Bear
REALISTIC FICTION *Ben Mikaelsen*

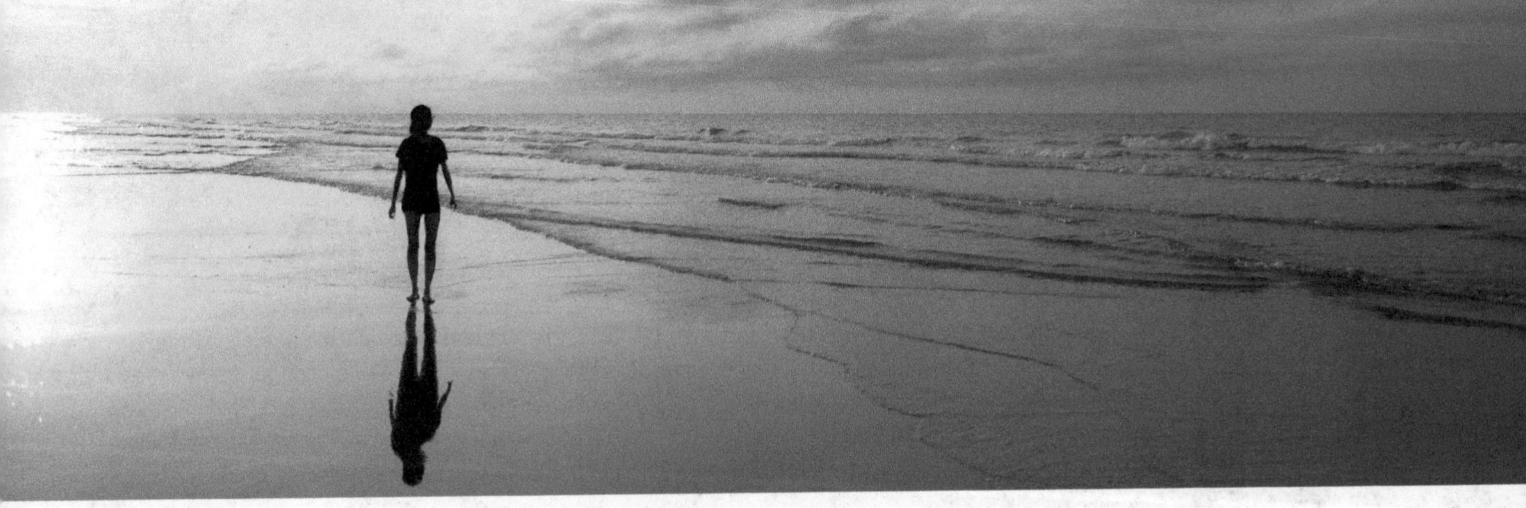

Extended Writing Project: Research Writing

97 **Plan**

Planning Research
Evaluating Sources
Research and Note-Taking

112 **Draft**

Critiquing Research
Paraphrasing
Sources and Citations
Print and Graphic Features

128 **Revise**

130 **Edit and Publish**

English Language Learner Resources

132 **Middle School Loneliness**
FICTION

141 **Shakespeare in Harlem**
INFORMATIONAL TEXT

151 Text Fulfillment through StudySync

Please note that excerpts and passages in the StudySync® library and this workbook are intended as touchstones to generate interest in an author's work. The excerpts and passages do not substitute for the reading of entire texts, and StudySync® strongly recommends that students seek out and purchase the whole literary or informational work in order to experience it as the author intended. Links to online resellers are available in our digital library. In addition, complete works may be ordered through an authorized reseller by filling out and returning to StudySync® the order form enclosed in this workbook.

Unit 6: True to Yourself

Who are you meant to be?

SVETLANA CHMAKOVA

Svetlana Chmakova (b. 1979) was born and raised in Russia, where she lived until the age of sixteen. Her family then moved to Canada, and Chmakova began to make stories in the form of manga, the Japanese style of narrative comics and graphic novels. She spends her time in both Canada and California, and publishes books about middle schoolers in the throes of everything from daily drama to epic battles against dark forces. Chmakova likes to draw ideas for characters from people-watching on the subway.

RITA DOVE

In 1993, the Library of Congress appointed Rita Dove (b. 1952) United States Poet Laureate, making Dove not only the youngest poet to ever be presented with the title, but also the first woman and first African American to hold the position. Dove, who lives and works in Virginia, has authored short stories, a novel, a play, essays, and many books of poetry. Her Pulitzer Prize–winning collection *Thomas and Beulah* (1986) is a sequence of poems based on the lives of her grandparents.

W.E.B. DUBOIS

"Either the United States will destroy ignorance or ignorance will destroy the United States," stated W. E. B. Du Bois (1868–1963) in a speech. The words and writings of this prolific activist, writer, historian, and professor continue to influence the fields of sociology and political science today. Du Bois was the first African American to earn a doctorate at Harvard University, and was a co-founder of the National Association for the Advancement of Colored People (NAACP) in 1909.

RUSSELL FREEDMAN

Russell Freedman (1929–2018) was born into a literary family—his father worked in a publishing house and his mother worked in a bookstore. After returning from service in the Korean War, Freedman became a reporter and editor for the Associated Press. His first book was *Teenagers Who Made History* (1961), a collection of stories of notable teenagers, and thereafter he wrote many historically focused books and biographies about individuals who created significant inventions or showed courage through difficult circumstances.

HENRY FORD

Before becoming one of the foremost pioneers of the industrial world, Henry Ford (1863–1947) was a rebellious child. At the age of sixteen, Ford left home to become a machine-maker's apprentice in Detroit. This early passion for industry eventually led him to develop his first automobile, which he termed the "Quadricycle", in 1896. The rest, as they say, is history. Ford's Model T car and the assembly line that made its mass production possible in 1908 became the basis for personal transportation and industrial manufacturing ever since.

NIKKI GRIMES

Born and raised in New York City, Nikki Grimes (b. 1950) began writing poems at the age of six and has been a writer ever since. "Books were my survival tools," she said of her childhood. "They were how I got by, and how I coped with things. Books carried me away." An author of poetry and fiction for both children and adults, Grimes has taught at schools in Sweden, Tanzania, Russia, and China. Her artistic talents are not limited to writing, Grimes has also performed as a singer and dancer, exhibited photographs, and crafted jewelry.

REBECCA HARRINGTON

Since her undergraduate years at the University of Minnesota–Twin Cities, Rebecca Harrington has pursued her joint interests of science and journalism. Beginning her career writing for the *Minnesota Daily*, Harrington went on to receive her Master's degree in the Science, Health and Environmental Reporting Program at New York University. Since then, she has covered topics such as rocket launches, solar energy, and the Zika virus for various magazines and newspapers.

JACKIE ROBINSON

Brooklyn Dodgers baseball player Jackie Robinson (1919–1972) made history in 1947 when he walked onto the field as the first African American player in the MLB in the 20th century. His ten-year career saw a World Series Championship win for the Dodgers, and earned Robinson a place in the National Baseball Hall of Fame in 1962. Martin Luther King Jr. called Robinson "a legend and symbol in his own time," as his accomplishments reached far beyond the baseball diamond, calling attention to the value and urgency of integration.

AMANDA SPERBER

Amanda Sperber (b. 1986) is an American journalist from Mamaroneck, New York, who splits time between Kenya, Somalia, and the United States. Sperber primarily covers stories that focus on conflict, crises, and developments in East African countries. Early in her career as a reporter, Sperber traveled and volunteered around the world, opening herself to new perspectives and ways of communicating in such places as Ghana, the West Indies, and the United Kingdom.

BEN MIKAELSEN

Many photographs of the Bolivian American author Ben Mikaelsen (b. 1952) also include a 750-pound black bear named Buffy. Mikaelsen rescued Buffy when he was a cub, and they shared a home in Montana—inside and outside—as family for twenty-six years. Growing up in Bolivia, Mikaelsen, who has always loved caring for animals, had many pets: dogs and cats, a sloth, and even a pet kudamundi. His novels often focus on the relationship between humankind and nature.

Bronx Masquerade

FICTION
Nikki Grimes
2002

Introduction

The teenage narrators of this highly acclaimed novel by American author and poet Nikki Grimes (b. 1950) have no outlet for expression until they come together in Mr. Ward's high school English class. Provided an opportunity to read their poems and lyrics to the class on popular "open mike" Fridays, the voices of the students intertwine to produce a powerful message of identity and awareness. Two of them, Devon and Janelle, are featured in this excerpt.

"But what about the rest of me? Forget who I really am, who I really want to be."

NOTES

Devon Hope

1 Jump Shot. What kind of name is that? Not mine, but try telling that to the brothers at school. That's all they ever call me.

2 You'd think it was written somewhere. Tall guys must be jocks[1]. No. Make that tall *people*, 'cause Diondra's got the same problem. Everybody expects her to shoot hoops. The difference is, she's got no talent in that direction. Ask me, she's got no business playing b-ball. That's my game.

3 I've got good height and good hands, and that's a fact. But what about the rest of me? Forget who I really am, who I really want to be. The law is be cool, be tough, play ball, and use books for weight training—not reading. Otherwise, everybody gives you grief. Don't ask me why I care, especially when the grief is coming from a punk like Wesley. Judging from the company he keeps, he's a gangsta in sheep's clothing[2]. I don't even know why he and Tyrone **bother** coming to school. It's clear they don't take it seriously, although maybe they're starting to. That's according to Sterling, who believes in praying for everybody and giving them the **benefit** of the doubt. I love the preacher-man, but I think he may be giving these brothers too much credit. Anyway, when I hang around after school and any of the guys ask me, "Yo, Devon, where are you going?" I tell them I'm heading for the gym to meet Coach and work on my layup. Then once they're out the door, I cut upstairs to the library to sneak a read.

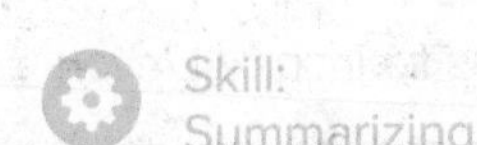
Skill: Summarizing

Overall, it seems like Devon's peers are not seeing his true self. I would summarize these paragraphs by saying: Although Devon likes basketball, he has other interests that define his character.

I wonder if these details will contribute to the overarching summary.

4 It's not much better at home. My older brother's always after me to hit the streets with him, calls me a girly man for loving books and jazz[3].

5 Don't get me wrong. B-ball is all right. Girls like you, for one thing. But it's not *you* they like. It's Mr. Basketball. And if that's not who you are inside, then it's not you they're liking. So what's the point? Still, I don't mind playing, just not all the time.

---

1. **jocks** athletic young men, generally assumed to be popular
2. **gangsta in sheep's clothing** a play on the idiom "wolf in sheep's clothing," referring to someone (or something) who hides their true intentions
3. **jazz** a type of music of African American origin characterized by improvisation, emerging at the beginning of the 20th century

NOTES

6 This year is looking better. My English teacher has got us studying the Harlem Renaissance, which means we have to read a lot of poetry. That suits me just fine, gives me a reason to drag around my beat-up **volumes** of Langston Hughes and Claude McKay. Whenever anybody bugs me about it, all I have to say is "Homework." Even so, I'd rather the brothers not catch me with my head in a book.

7 The other day, I duck into the library, **snare** a corner table, and hunker down with *3000 Years of Black Poetry*. Raynard sees me, but it's not like he's going to tell anybody. He hardly speaks, and he never hangs with any of the brothers I know. So I breathe easy. I'm sure no one else has spotted me until a head pops up from behind the stacks. It's Janelle Battle from my English class. I freeze and wait for the **snickers** I'm used to. Wait for her to say something like: "What? Coach got you *reading* now? Afraid you're gonna flunk out and drop off the team?" But all she does is smile and wave. Like it's no big deal for me to be in a library reading. Like I have a right to be there if I want. Then she pads over, slips a copy of *The Panther & the Lash* on my table, and walks away without saying a word. It's one of my favorite books by Langston Hughes. How could she know? Seems like she's noticed me in the library more often than I thought.

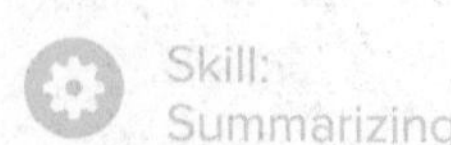
Skill: Summarizing

In this section, Janelle seems to inspire Devon to be true to himself. Here is how I would summarize this paragraph: Janelle's independence motivates Devon to begin thinking differently about how he acts; he wants to start being himself.

8 Janelle is all right. So what if she's a little plump? At least when you turn the light on upstairs, somebody's home. She's smart, and she doesn't try hiding it. Which gets me thinking. Maybe it's time I quit sneaking in and out of the library like some thief. Maybe it's time I just started being who I am.

9 Open Mike
Bronx Masquerade
By Devon Hope

I woke up this morning
exhausted from hiding
the me of me
*so I stand here **confiding***
there's more to Devon
than jump shot and rim.
I'm more than tall
and lengthy of limb.
I dare you to peep
behind these eyes,
discover the poet
in tough-guy disguise.
Don't call me Jump Shot.
My name is Surprise.

NOTES

Janelle Battle

10 "Janelle Hope. Mrs. Janelle Hope. Mrs. Devon Hope." Dream on, fool. You can stand here in the girls' room and practice saying that name 'til your tongue falls out, or the change bell rings, whichever comes first, and it still won't ever be true. Face it. Devon is Denzel Washington, and you are Thighs "R" Us.

11 I can hear Lupe now. "Stop putting yourself down. You have a very pretty face. Besides, you have a lot more going for you." Yeah, well, I guess that's true. I mean, I am smart and funny, and I know I'm a good person. But this is high school, and nobody seems to care about that. Why couldn't I be tall and elegant like Diondra, or have Judianne's perfect **complexion**, all smooth, super-rich fudge? Better yet, why couldn't I look like Tanisha, or Gloria? Then I might have a chance with somebody like Devon. But I don't, so forget it.

12 Devon is different from the other jocks, though. How many guys you know read Claude McKay for fun? Seems like every time I go to the library, I catch him squeezed into a corner like he's got something to hide. He smiled at me last time I saw him there. That's something, isn't it? He didn't have to smile, even if I did smile and wave first. And he seemed to like the poem I read at the last Open Mike Friday.

13 I can't believe I'm getting up in front of people and talking about personal stuff, and liking it. I'm saying things that I would never tell anybody, usually. But, I don't know. There's something about reading poetry. It's almost like acting. The room is kind of set up like a stage, anyway. Mr. Ward turns most of the lights out, and we stand in a spot in front of the video camera. Once he switches it on, it's like you become somebody else, and you can say anything, as long as it's in a poem. Then, when you're finished, you just disappear into the dark and sit down, and you're back to being your own self. Gloria says it's the same for her.

14 "Hey, Janelle."

15 Oh, no. It's Miss Big Mouth Fifth Avenue in another one of her original getups. Where'd she come from?

16 "Hey, Judianne." I thought the bathroom was empty. How long was she there? I hope she didn't hear me talking to the mirror. That's all I need, to have the whole school laughing about me having a crush on Devon. Lord, please don't let that happen. It's bad enough they call me Battle of the Bulge behind my back.

17 I wish, I wish, I wish. God, I wish people could see me on the inside. I know I'm beautiful there.

18 Open Mike
Inside
By Janelle Battle

Daily
I notice you frown
at my thick casing,
feel you poke me
with the sharp tip
of your booted words.
You laugh,
rap my woody shell
with wicked whispers shaped
like knuckles,
then toss me aside.
Lucky for me,
I don't bruise easily.
Besides,
your loss
is someone else's gain
for I am coconut,
and the heart of me
is sweeter
than you know.

Excerpted from *Bronx Masquerade* by Nikki Grimes, published by Dial Books.

First Read

Read *Bronx Masquerade*. After you read, complete the Think Questions below.

 THINK QUESTIONS

1. How does Devon feel about his nickname? Respond with evidence from the text.

2. Why does Devon hide his true interests? Cite evidence from the text to support your response.

3. What social pressures does Janelle face? Be sure to refer back to the text in your response.

4. Use context to determine the meaning of the word **volumes** as it is used in paragraph 6. Write your definition of *volumes* here and explain how you arrived at it.

5. Use context to determine the meaning of the word **snickers** as it is used in paragraph 7. Write your definition here and identify clues that helped you figure out its meaning. Then check the meaning in a dictionary.

Skill: Summarizing

Use the Checklist to analyze Summarizing in *Bronx Masquerade*. Refer to the sample student annotations about Summarizing in the text.

••• CHECKLIST FOR SUMMARIZING

In order to determine how to write an objective summary of a text, note the following:

- ✓ in a nonfiction text, examine details to identify the main idea, making notations in a notebook or graphic organizer
- ✓ in literature, note the setting, characters, and events in the plot, including the problem the characters face and how it is solved
- ✓ answers to the basic questions *who, what, where, when, why,* and *how*
- ✓ stay objective, and do not add your own personal thoughts, judgments, or opinions to the summary

To provide an objective summary of a text free from personal opinions or judgments, consider the following questions:

- ✓ What are the answers to basic *who, what, where, when, why,* and *how* questions in literature and works of nonfiction?
- ✓ Are all of the details I have summarized in a work of literature related to the theme?
- ✓ In what order should I put the main ideas and most important details in a work of nonfiction to make my summary logical?
- ✓ Is my summary objective, or have I added my own thoughts, judgments, or personal opinions?

Skill: Summarizing

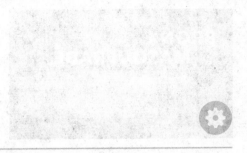

Reread paragraphs 16–19 of *Bronx Masquerade*. Then, using the Checklist on the previous page, answer the multiple-choice questions below.

YOUR TURN

1. Which sentence provides the BEST objective summary of paragraph 16?

   - O A. Janelle sees Judianne in the bathroom in the library. She is surprised to see her and wishes she would leave.
   - O B. Judianne enters the bathroom while Janelle is talking in the mirror. Janelle is embarrassed as she thinks she may be bullied.
   - O C. Janelle is in the bathroom in the library when Judianne walks in. Earlier that day, Janelle has been ruthlessly bullied by her peers.
   - O D. Judianne hears Janelle talking to herself in the bathroom about wanting to date Devon. She makes fun of Janelle.

2. Which of the following answers provides the BEST objective summary of Janelle's poem in paragraph 18?

   - O A. Janelle is bullied by her peers at school, but she doesn't let it get to her because she believes she has more to offer than just looks.
   - O B. Janelle pretends not to hear her peers' unkind words. She thinks there is more to life than appearance.
   - O C. Janelle's life at school is rough. She wishes people could see the real her.
   - O D. Janelle's peers are aggressive toward her at school. Her poetry is a way to cope with their bullying.

Close Read

Reread *Bronx Masquerade*. As you reread, complete the Skills Focus questions below. Then use your answers and annotations from the questions to help you complete the Write activity.

SKILLS FOCUS

1. Create an objective summary of Devon's "Open Mike" poem. Include textual evidence to support your summary.

2. Read the following dictionary entry:

   direction

   di•rec•tion \də-'rek-shən\

   Noun

   1. a course along which something moves
   2. general aim or purpose
   3. an authoritative command
   4. instructions on how to accomplish a task or goal

   Which definition most closely matches the meaning of **direction** as it is used in paragraph 2? Write the appropriate definition of *direction* here and explain how you figured out the correct meaning.

3. Using evidence from the text, explain how the author develops the points of view of Devon and Janelle, and note how their points of view differ in their poems.

4. Explain how Devon and Janelle are true to themselves, despite feeling pressure from their peers. Use textual evidence to support your explanation.

WRITE

DISCUSSION: In *Bronx Masquerade*, Devon and Janelle are ready for their classmates to know who they truly are. Do you think that Devon and Janelle can be accepted for who they really are by their peers? Do you think they can help each other? Why or why not? Summarize Devon and Janelle's experiences with each other and with their peers to plan for a debate. Use evidence from the text to support your position.

A BEACON of Hope:

The Story of Hannah Herbst

INFORMATIONAL TEXT

Rebecca Harrington

2015

Introduction

The Discovery Education 3M Young Scientist Challenge has a simple mission: "to foster a new generation of American scientists at an age when interest in science generally declines." To enter, students from around the country (grades 5–8) are encouraged to submit a solution to a problem facing either them, their community, or the world at large. Each finalist gets the opportunity to work directly with a scientist in the hopes of bringing their idea to fruition. The 2015 winner was then-eighth-grader Hannah Herbst from Boca Raton, Florida. The problem she wanted to solve: the global energy crisis. Her solution: BEACON.

"I could use the skills I acquired to take action in an attempt to mitigate the global energy crisis."

1 In 2015, an eighth grader named Hannah Herbst from Boca Raton, Florida won the Discovery Education 3M Young Scientist Challenge.

2 At just 14 years old, she designed and built a small **turbine** called BEACON, for Bringing Electricity Access to Countries Through Ocean Energy Collection.

3 "Shortly after school began," Herbst wrote in a blog post for the contest, "I received a letter from my nine-year-old pen pal[1] in Ethiopia. She wrote about how she has no access to lights, a steady flow of fresh water to drink, and other basic necessities. I recognized that her situation was not unique and believed that I could use the skills I **acquired** to take action in an attempt to **mitigate** the global energy crisis."

4 So Hannah got to work on her ocean energy probe[2]. She spent four months researching her idea, she wrote in another blog post, before she designed the turbine as a computer model, and then produced 3D-printed **prototypes.** Herbst even got approval from the city of Boca Raton to test her design in the intercoastal waterway[3].

5 There, she explains in her contest entry video, the ocean tidal energy drives the propeller at the bottom of the probe, which then powers the hydroelectric generator[4] at the top of the probe via a pulley system inside, turning ocean tides into usable power.

6 Herbst's calculations show that if she scaled up BEACON, it could charge three car batteries **simultaneously** in less than an hour. She suggests the turbine could be used in developing countries to renewably power pumps to **desalinate** water, run centrifuges that help test blood for diseases, and power electric buoys for **maritime** navigation.

---

1. **pen pal** someone with whom correspondence is regularly exchanged
2. **probe** an instrument used for exploring hidden places in the environment
3. **intercoastal waterway** a 3,000-mile inland waterway along the Atlantic and Gulf of Mexico coasts of the United States
4. **generator** a machine that provides electricity via mechanical energy

7 Herbst became interested in science at an engineering camp during the summer before seventh grade. When she got there, she realized she was the only girl.

8 "I knew that I was the minority,"she wrote, "but after successfully programming and constructing robots that day, my love and passion for science and engineering was discovered."

9 And she hopes other young scientists will find their passion, too. "If you're reading this blog post and are in middle school, I hope that you will apply for the Discovery Education and 3M Young Scientist Challenge," Herbst wrote. "It is such an amazing opportunity to explore, **innovate**, and work with a scientist from 3M to develop your prototype. I hope to see YOU posting blogs next year!"

WRITE

PERSONAL RESPONSE: "A BEACON of Hope: The Story of Hannah Herbst" describes a teen's invention that could help power an entire nation. If you were to create an invention to help a nation in need, what would it be? Why? Support your response with evidence from the article as well as personal experience. As you make connections between Hannah's life and your own, include anything that may have impacted your ideas about your potential invention.

Shree Bose:

Never Too Young to Change the World

INFORMATIONAL TEXT

Amanda Sperber

2017

Introduction

Amanda Sperber is a freelance journalist who has lived and worked all over the world. In this article, she writes about Shree Bose, a cancer researcher who won the Grand Prize in the 2011 Google Science Fair. Bose was victorious out of 10,000 participants, ages 17 or 18, from 91 different countries around the world. Since receiving the honor, Bose has used her platform to encourage interest in STEM education and has continued her own education as well, graduating from Harvard University and beginning a MD/PhD program at Duke University School of Medicine.

"They all told her she was too young."

Turning Tragedy into Inspiration

1 When she was 15, Shree Bose traveled from her home in Fort Worth, Texas, to visit her grandfather in India. He was dying of cancer. Shree had been close to her grandfather even though she lived far away. "While I think the barrier of living on the other side of the world definitely **posed** a challenge to being able to talk as often as we would have liked, my grandfather was close to both my brother and me," Shree says. "He would visit when we were younger, and when we got a bit older and would travel to India, he would sit and talk with us for hours."

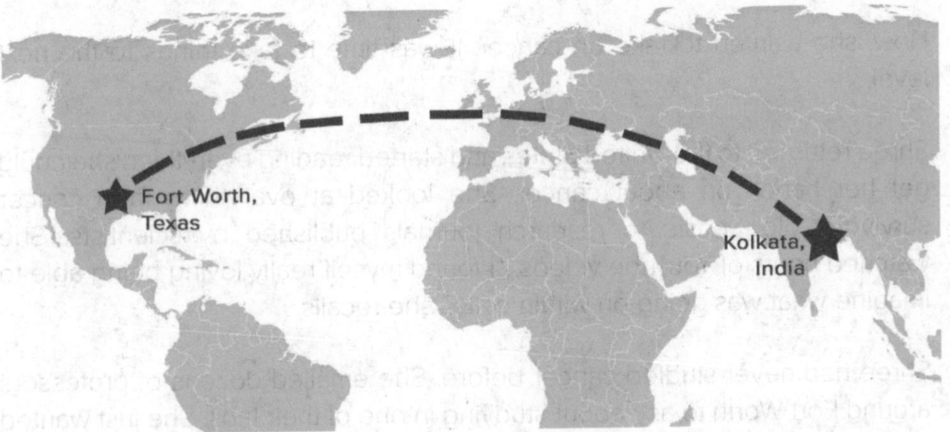

2 In Kolkata, a city in eastern India, Shree sat with her grandfather, and, seeing his discomfort, realized her purpose in life: she wanted to fight vicious diseases like cancer. She wanted to play a role in **relieving** people's pain. "When my grandfather passed away," Shree says, "it was the first time where I said, 'This is what I want to do with my life. This is what I want to make an impact in.'"

NOTES

Skill: Media

The section heading suggests an important event in Shree's life. The map emphasizes how far it was to visit her grandfather. From these details I conclude that her grandfather's illness was both a tragedy and an inspiration for Shree.

NOTES

3 Shree had always been creative. She enjoyed building things that solved problems or addressed issues she saw in her daily life. For example, in fifth grade she made a remote controlled garbage can that she thought might be helpful to disabled students struggling to take the garbage out to the curb.

4 Now, she wanted to take on cancer. It was time to take things to the next level.

5 Shree returned to the United States and started reading everything she could get her hands on about cancer. She looked at everything from cancer survivors' blog posts to research journals published by scientists. She watched hours of YouTube videos. "I found myself really loving being able to imagine what was going on within cells," she recalls.

6 Shree had never studied cancer before. She emailed dozens of professors around Fort Worth to ask about studying in one of their labs. She just wanted a chance to experiment and learn. They all told her she was too young. "I got **rejected** by a lot of professors before I found one person who was willing to take me on," she says.

7 That person was Dr. Alakananda Basu, a professor at the University of North Texas Health Science Center in Fort Worth. Although she was young and inexperienced, Shree won over Dr. Basu with her energy and passion for learning. "What I find most exciting is your enthusiasm," Shree says Dr. Basu told her. "And if you keep that while working in my lab, I'll take you."

8 Under Dr. Basu's **supervision**, Shree started research on counteracting resistance to the chemotherapy[1] drug cisplatin, which is given to women with ovarian cancer[2]. She also discovered a **unique** platform to share her research in 2011, the first year of the Google Science Fair. "They actually had a little banner ad [on the Google homepage]," she recalls. "And I remember I didn't think too much about it until my Dad mentioned it to me again."

9 The Google Science Fair is entirely online. Participants demonstrate their projects on websites they make themselves. Shree had never made a website, but she went for it and entered one. So did a lot of other students. In fact, 10,000 students from 91 countries submitted projects to the competition its first year.

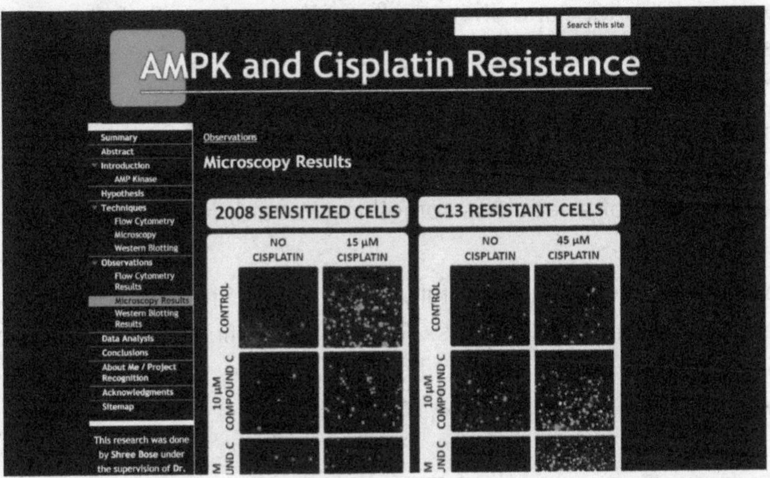

10 Shree won.

NOTES

Skill: Media

The website screenshot with this text shows how Shree's research results were displayed online. Without both features, Shree's work might be hard to understand.

1. **chemotherapy** a widely used treatment to prevent cancer cells from dividing and growing
2. **ovarian cancer** cancer that begins in one or more ovum

11 "I remember the entire experience as very much of a whirlwind that didn't feel real in a lot of ways. Even so many years later, that experience shaped the excitement with how I approach science and how I approach telling others about my work, and that's a blessing I'll take forward into my life," she says.

Starting Young

12 Shree was only six years old when she conducted her first experiment. Her first goal was to change vegetables into more interesting colors. She wanted to know if she would eat foods like spinach more often if they were more exciting colors. "It was very much like, 'I am very bored by the color, so if you make it bright and shiny I will put it in my mouth,'" she says of her first-grade project.

13 Her parents took her seriously. They bought her a spinach plant, blue food coloring, and a syringe to inject into the plant. "They had a big role in how I ended up thinking of science as something I could do," she says.

14 The spinach plant was successfully dyed blue. Shree forgot to water it, though, and it died in two weeks. "That was my first science project," she says. She took the dead plant to her first science fair in second grade. "I actually think I got laughed at," she recalls.

15 Despite the setback, she continued to allow her interests to lead her. Her technique improved with time. She completed projects like the electronic garbage can, for which Shree won a regional award. She also developed a traction pad to help cars get out of the mud when she was in sixth grade.

16 And, of course, she later became a Google Science Fair champion. Winning that competition changed Shree's life. She met President Barack Obama. *Glamour* magazine named her one of its '21 Amazing Young Women of the Year'. She received emails from all around the country from cancer patients and their family members.

17 The most important change, though, was in how Shree saw herself. "Before, the judges seemed practically superhuman, like nothing a regular kid from Texas could aspire to be," she wrote in a 2012 article in the Huffington Post titled, "How the Google Science Fair Changed My Life." "When I met them in person, I realized that they were just really intelligent and really hard-working — the kind of person everyone has the potential to become. Those are the people who are out there changing the world."

Inspiring the Next Shree Bose

18 Shree's youthful involvement in science isn't just important because of her incredible achievements. It is important because participation in science is not as common in young women as it is in young men. Fewer young women engaging in science, technology, engineering, and math (otherwise known as STEM) as youths means fewer girls will become women with jobs in STEM. Statistics support this: according to the National Girls Collaborative Project, women make up just 29% of the science and engineering workforce.

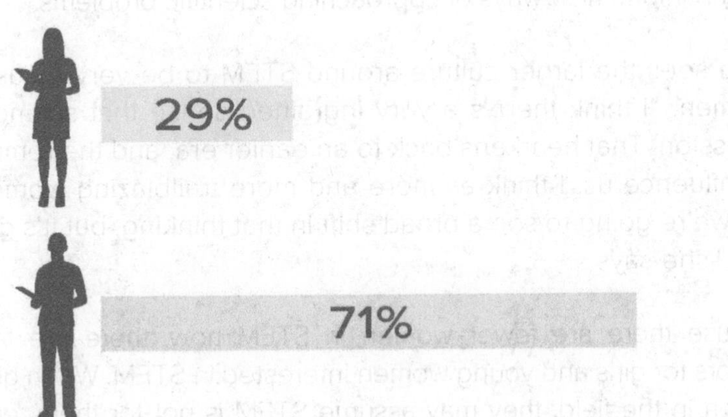

NOTES

19 There are currently more jobs in STEM fields than in any other industry. For example, the National Council for Women and Information Technology (NCWIT) estimates that there will be around 1.4 million computer specialist job openings expected in the U.S. by 2018. Americans need to fill those jobs, and the best bet to make the best products is to fill at least half of these jobs with women.

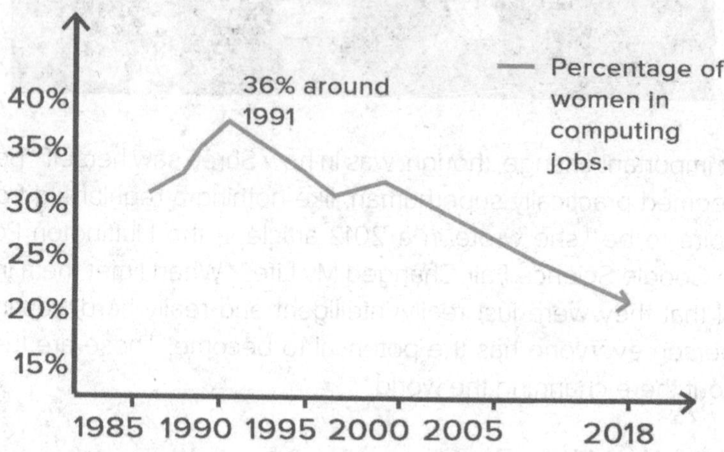

Skill:
Word Meaning

I am not sure what the word ingrained means, but I can tell it's an adjective because it is describing sense. She is describing the sense that science is a male profession. Maybe it means large or popular?

The second meaning makes no sense in this sentence! The first does, and even though my guesses were wrong they are kind of close. Firmly fixed means a lot of people think that way and will have a hard time changing their minds.

20 Science, engineering, and technology jobs impact our everyday lives. "I think any societal barriers to that pioneering spirit, whether gender or otherwise, puts the world at a disadvantage, since there are so many more discoveries waiting to be made," Shree says.

21 Shree believes STEM fields would benefit from having more women involved. As she says, "I think it's absolutely essential for women to be in STEM, not just because of the obvious reasons that we can be and equality is good for society, but also because women have unique perspectives and experiences that can inform new ways of approaching scientific problems."

22 Shree sees the larger culture around STEM to be very focused on boys and men. "I think there's a very ingrained sense that science is a male profession. That hearkens back to an earlier era, and the remnants of that still influence us. I think as more and more trailblazing women pave the way, we're going to see a broad shift in that thinking, but it's going to take work," she says.

23 Because there are fewer women in STEM now, there are fewer female mentors for girls and young women interested in STEM. When girls don't see women in the field, they may assume STEM is not for them, either. "I have

NOTES

been fortunate to have some incredible female mentors and role models, and I think that their examples have taught me to think in innovative ways and push the boundaries of scientific inquiry," Shree says.

24 After winning the Google Science Fair in 2011, Shree enrolled at Harvard University. At Harvard, she mentored young people. They often asked how she got started in STEM. She would tell them about doing research, finding Dr. Basu, and getting involved in a lab for hands-on experience. However, she didn't have suggestions about how to get started with the "E" in STEM: engineering. Shree knew engineering could be interesting and fun, but she didn't have a way to show that to the students she mentored. So, once again, after defining a problem, Shree Bose came up with a solution.

25 She and two colleagues built Piper, a toolkit that allows users to build electronics and gadgets while they play Minecraft. Piper comes in a box as a completely unassembled computer. Young people put it together themselves and then link their own computer using a small microchip. With that, they can upgrade the unit with physical wires and switches so they can handle each piece and understand how the parts make up a whole. The goal is to engage young people in the nuts and bolts, so to speak, of the engineering process.

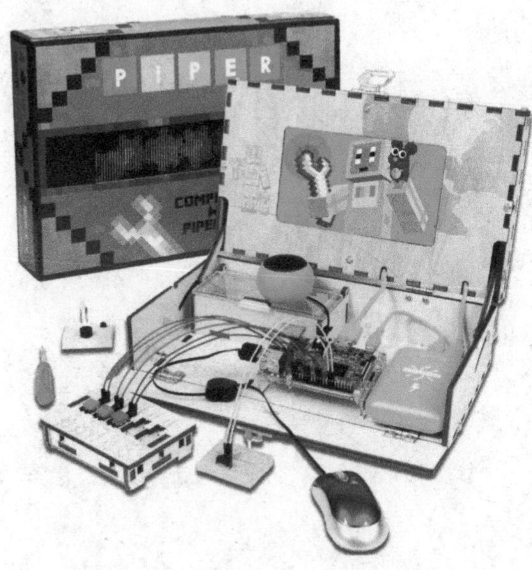

26 Shree earned her undergraduate degree from Harvard in 2016. She's continuing her education, at Duke University School of Medicine in Durham, North Carolina. In medical school she rotates quickly through different specialities. "I'm learning a lot really quickly," she says of the experience.

27 When she finishes at Duke, Shree hopes to work as a pediatric oncologist, taking care of kids with blood diseases and cancer. For now, though, she's open to all possibilities and to whatever opportunities come her way. "We'll see," she says. "Check back in with me in seven years!"

AMANDA SPERBER is an East Africa-based foreign correspondent. She files for Al Jazeera, The Daily Beast, New Foreign Policy, Glamour, The Guardian, Harper's, News Deeply, The Times of London, VICE Magazine and related publications.

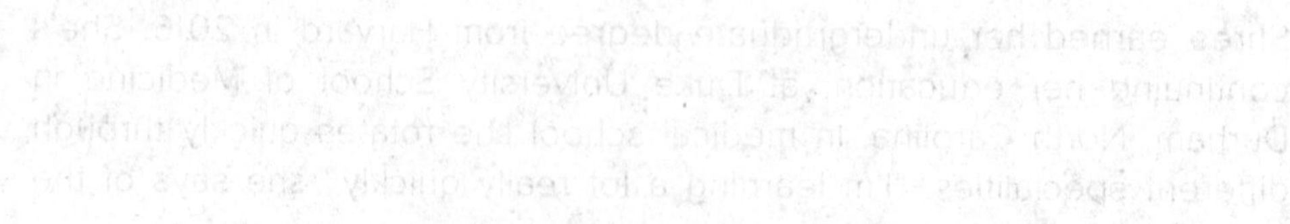

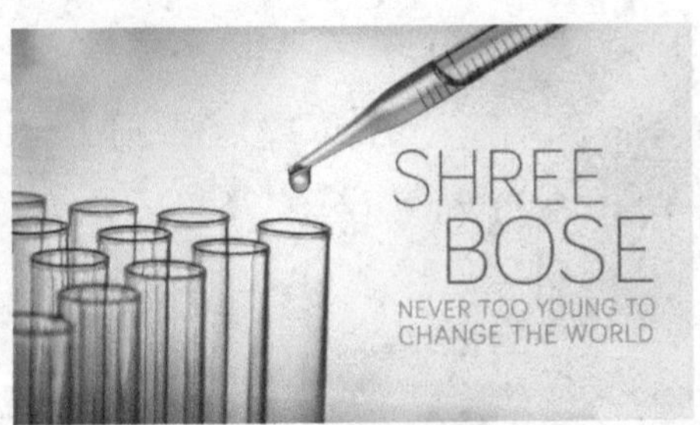

First Read

Read "Shree Bose: Never Too Young to Change the World." After you read, complete the Think Questions below.

THINK QUESTIONS

1. What was Shree Bose's first experiment? Explain how the same qualities she showed in conducting this first experiment have continued throughout her scientific career, citing textual evidence to support your answer.

2. Who was one of the most important people to help Shree Bose discover her understanding of science? Explain this mentor's role, citing specific textual evidence in your response.

3. How did the Google Science Fair change Shree Bose's life? How did it change her perspective on the world? Be sure to include textual evidence or inferences in your response.

4. Read the following dictionary entry:

   relieve

   re•lieve /rə'lēv/

   verb

   1. to cause pain or difficulty to become less serious
   2. to release someone from duty by taking their place
   3. to take a burden from someone

   Which definition most closely matches the meaning of the word **relieving** as it is used in the text? Write the correct definition, and describe how you know which meaning of *relieving* fits in the text.

5. Which neighboring words and phrases help you determine the meaning of **unique** as it is used in the text? Write your own definition of *unique*, and explain how you were able to determine the meaning through context. Then use a dictionary to confirm your conclusion.

Skill: Media

Use the Checklist to analyze Media in "Shree Bose: Never Too Young to Change the World." Refer to the sample student annotations about Media in the text.

••• CHECKLIST FOR MEDIA

In order to determine how to compare and contrast reading a story, drama, or poem with "experiencing it though different media formats, such as graphs, charts, and other visual aids and devices, do the following:

- ✓ choose a story that has been presented in different media formats, such as graphs, charts, and other visual aids and devices
- ✓ think about the key features of the different media presentations
- ✓ consider how different kinds of media treat story elements in different ways
- ✓ think about what you "see", or imagine, when you read a story and how it compares with what you see, or imagine, when you experience the story through graphs, charts, and other visual aids and devices

To compare and contrast the experience of reading a story, drama, or poem to experiencing it by viewing different media formats, such as graphs, charts, and other visual aids and devices, consider the following questions:

- ✓ What features of each medium are the most important?
- ✓ How do different media formats, such as graphs, charts, and other visual aids and devices affect the written work?
- ✓ How is the way you picture a character in your mind affected when you see that same character portrayed in an illustration?

Skill: Media

Reread paragraphs 18–19 from "Shree Bose: Never Too Young to Change the World." Then, using the Checklist on the previous page, answer the multiple-choice questions below.

YOUR TURN

1. The heading suggests that this section will be about —

   - ○ A. finding a researcher to replace Shree Bose.
   - ○ B. how to interest other young women in science.
   - ○ C. ways to teach science in schools.
   - ○ D. finding young women to compete in science fairs.

2. The purpose of the first visual in the excerpt is to —

   - ○ A. show that the number of women in STEM jobs is increasing.
   - ○ B. illustrate the future projected number of men and women in STEM jobs.
   - ○ C. illustrate the difference in the number of women and men in STEM jobs.
   - ○ D. show the employment opportunities available for women in STEM jobs.

3. The second chart illustrates the author's ideas in paragraph 19 by showing that —

   - ○ A. at least 50% of the computing jobs available in 2018 will be filled by women because of the NCWIT.
   - ○ B. there will be no women in computing jobs by 2018 unless something is done to stop the decline.
   - ○ C. there will not be enough women in computing to fill half the number of computing jobs available by 2018.
   - ○ D. many of the computing jobs available in 2018 will go unfilled because fewer women are entering computing.

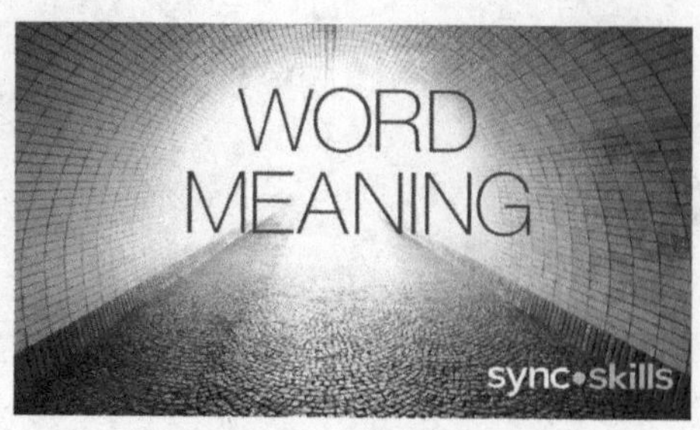

Skill: Word Meaning

Use the Checklist to analyze Word Meaning in "Shree Bose: Never Too Young to Change the World." Refer to the sample student annotations about Word Meaning in the text.

••• CHECKLIST FOR WORD MEANING

In order to find the pronunciation of a word or determine or clarify its precise meaning or its part of speech, do the following:

- ✓ determine the word's part of speech
- ✓ consult reference materials, both print and digital, to find the pronunciation of a word, determine its precise meaning and ascertain its part of speech

In order to verify the preliminary determination of the meaning of a word or phrase, do the following:

- ✓ use context clues to make an inference of the word's meaning
- ✓ consult a dictionary to verify your preliminary determination of the meaning
- ✓ be sure to read all of the definitions, and then decide which definition makes sense in its context

To determine a word's precise meaning or part of speech, ask the following questions:

- ✓ What is the word describing?
- ✓ How is the word being used in the phrase or sentence?
- ✓ Have I consulted my reference materials?

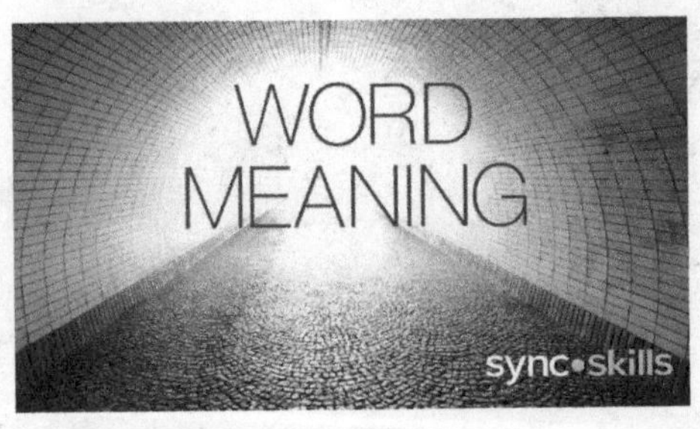

Skill: Word Meaning

Reread paragraphs 11–15 from "Shree Bose: Never Too Young to Change the World." Then, using the Checklist on the previous page, answer the multiple-choice questions below.

YOUR TURN

1. Which definition best matches the way the word *whirlwind* is used in paragraph 11? Remember to pay attention to the word's part of speech as you make your decision.

   - A. Definition 1
   - B. Definition 2
   - C. Definition 3
   - D. Definition 4

2. Which definition best matches the way the word *setback* is used in paragraph 15?

   - A. Definition 1
   - B. Definition 2
   - C. Definition 3
   - D. Definition 4

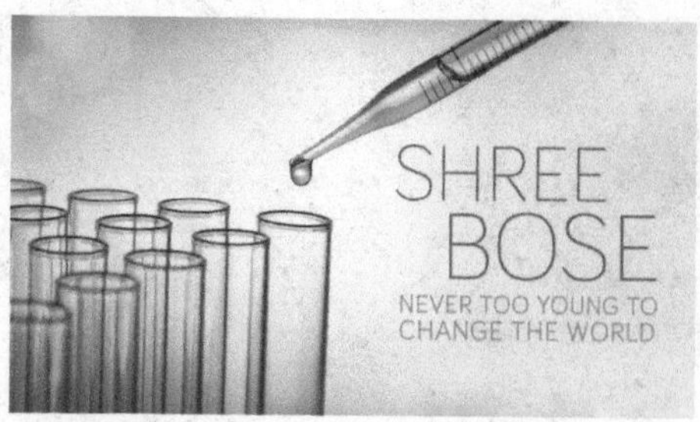

Close Read

Reread "Shree Bose: Never Too Young to Change the World." As you reread, complete the Skills Focus questions below. Then use your answers and annotations from the questions to help you complete the Write activity.

SKILLS FOCUS

1. Identify examples of the author's use of visuals to present information about Shree's scientific approach to problem-solving. Explain how the visuals help you understand Shree's approach.

2. Identify evidence that supports the author's central idea that Shree Bose is a problem-solver. Explain how the evidence helps further to explain the central idea.

3. Highlight examples in the text where the author uses different media or formats as well as words to help readers understand the author's concern about the number of women in STEM fields. Explain how the information helps illustrate the problem.

4. Use context clues to make your best guess at the definition of *equality* as it is used in paragraph 21. After you've guessed, look up *equality* in the dictionary and determine the correct definition in this context.

5. Highlight evidence in the text that explains how Shree Bose answered the unit's essential question: Who are you meant to be? Find evidence in the text to support your answer.

WRITE

INFORMATIVE: What qualities make a great problem-solver? You read that Hannah Herbst set out to solve the global energy crisis to help her pen pal in Ethiopia. How does Shree Bose find solutions to scientific and everyday problems she has encountered throughout her life? How does the author's use of information presented in different media or formats as well as in words help illustrate Shree's scientific approach to finding solutions? Use evidence from both the text and charts, visuals, or other quantitative information to support your ideas.

Letter to His Daughter

INFORMATIONAL TEXT

W.E.B. Du Bois

1914

Introduction

W.E.B. Du Bois (1868–1963) was one of the cofounders of the National Association for the Advancement of Colored People (NAACP), a writer, a civil rights activist, and the first African American man to earn a PhD from Harvard. The letter here is of a personal nature: when she was fourteen, Du Bois's daughter, Yolande, crossed the ocean to study at Bedales School in England. In this letter to her, Du Bois cautions her of the strange and wonderful things she might encounter in this new place, and imparts his own practical advice about how to meet the challenges ahead.

"Remember that most folk laugh at anything unusual, whether it is beautiful, fine or not."

New York, October 29, 1914

Dear Little Daughter:

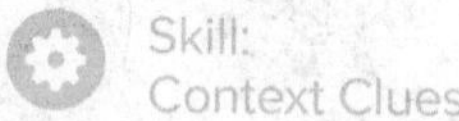

What does "gradually" mean? in paragraph 2 I see that this word is an adverb because it ends in -ly. It must describe something. Maybe time? This explains that Du Bois thinks his daughter will love the old world over time. Does "gradually" mean happening slowly over a period of time?

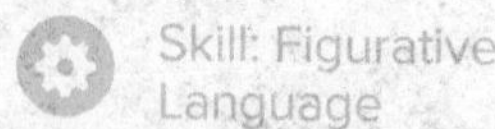

Du Bois compares new experiences with a cold bath and a big bedroom. The comparisons connect something new with something familiar. The author wants to express that bravery is required in her situation.

1 I have waited for you to get well settled before writing. By this time I hope some of the strangeness has worn off and that my little girl is working hard and regularly.

2 Of course, everything is new and unusual. You miss the newness and smartness of America. Gradually, however, you are going to sense the beauty of the old world: its calm and eternity and you will grow to love it.

3 Above all remember, dear, that you have a great opportunity. You are in one of the world's best schools, in one of the world's greatest modern empires. Millions of boys and girls all over this world would give almost anything they possess to be where you are. You are there by no **desert** or **merit** of yours, but only by lucky chance.

4 Deserve it, then. Study, do your work. Be honest, frank and fearless and get some grasp of the real values of life. You will meet, of course, curious little annoyances. People will wonder at your dear brown and the sweet **crinkley** hair. But that simply is of no importance and will soon be forgotten. Remember that most folk laugh at anything unusual, whether it is beautiful, fine or not. You, however, must not laugh at yourself. You must know that brown is as pretty as white or prettier and crinkley hair as straight even though it is harder to comb. The main thing is the YOU beneath the clothes and skin—the ability to do, the will to **conquer**, the determination to understand and know this great, wonderful, curious world. Don't shrink from new experiences and custom. Take the cold bath bravely. Enter into the spirit of your big bed-room. Enjoy what is and not **pine** for what is not. Read some good, heavy, serious books just for discipline: Take yourself in hand and **master** yourself. Make yourself do unpleasant things, so as to gain the upper hand of your soul.

NOTES

5 Above all remember: your father loves you and believes in you and expects you to be a wonderful woman.

6 I shall write each week and expect a weekly letter from you.

Lovingly yours,
Papa

First Read

Read "Letter to His Daughter." After you read, complete the Think Questions below.

THINK QUESTIONS

1. Why do you think W.E.B. Du Bois decided to write this letter to his daughter? Cite evidence from the letter in your response.

2. In paragraph 4, Du Bois offers his daughter some words of encouragement as she begins a new chapter of her life. Citing examples from the text, explain what he thinks is most important for his daughter to remember.

3. What does W.E.B. Du Bois's letter to his daughter tell you about him as a father? Cite specific examples from the text to support your analysis.

4. In paragraph 4, which context clues help you determine the definition of the word **pine**? Write your best definition of the word *pine* and explain how you inferred its meaning.

5. Read the following dictionary entry:

   master
   mas•ter \mastər\

   noun

   1. a man who has people working for him
   2. a person skilled in a particular art or profession

   verb

   1. to gain control of or overcome
   2. to learn a skill or trade thoroughly

   adjective

   1. having great skill or proficiency

   Which definition most closely matches the meaning of **master** in paragraph 4? Write the correct definition of *master* here and explain how you figured it out.

Skill: Figurative Language

Use the Checklist to analyze Figurative Language in "Letter to His Daughter." Refer to the sample student annotations about Figurative Language in the text.

••• CHECKLIST FOR FIGURATIVE LANGUAGE

To determine the meaning of figures of speech in a text, note the following:

- ✓ words that mean one thing literally and suggest something else
- ✓ similes, such as "strong as an ox"
- ✓ metaphors, such as "her eyes were stars"
- ✓ personification, such as "the daisies danced in the wind"

In order to interpret the meaning of a figure of speech in context, ask the following questions:

- ✓ Does any of the descriptive language in the text compare two seemingly unlike things?
- ✓ Do any descriptions include "like" or "as" that indicate a simile?
- ✓ Is there a direct comparison that suggests a metaphor?
- ✓ Is a human quality used to describe an animal, object, force of nature or idea that suggests personification?
- ✓ How does the use of this figure of speech change your understanding of the thing or person being described?

Skill: Figurative Language

Reread paragraph 4 from "Letter to His Daughter." Then, using the Checklist on the previous page, answer the multiple-choice questions below.

YOUR TURN

1. What does the idiom "gain the upper hand" mean?

   - A. to take control
   - B. to beat someone in a fight
   - C. to wrestle with someone
   - D. to raise one's hand

2. For what purpose does Du Bois use figures of speech in this passage?

   - A. They show Du Bois will punish his daughter if she doesn't succeed.
   - B. They show Du Bois does not have faith in his daughter's skills.
   - C. They show Du Bois thinks his daughter has the power to take control over her own life.
   - D. They show Du Bois fears for his daughter's soul.

Skill: Context Clues

Use the Checklist to analyze Context Clues in "Letter to His Daughter." Refer to the sample student annotations about Context Clues in the text.

••• CHECKLIST FOR CONTEXT CLUES

In order to use context as a clue to infer the meaning of a word or phrase, note the following:

✓ clues about the word's part of speech

✓ clues in the surrounding text about the word's meaning

✓ signal words that cue a type of context clue, such as:

- *for example* or *for instance* to signal an example context clue
- *like, similarly,* or *just as* to signal a comparison clue
- *but, however,* or *unlike* to signal a contrast context clue

To determine the meaning of a word or phrase as it is used in a text, consider the following questions:

✓ What is the overall sentence, paragraph, or text about?

✓ How does the word function in the sentence?

✓ What clues can help me determine the word's part of speech?

✓ What text clues can help me figure out the word's definition?

✓ Are there any examples that show what the word means?

✓ What do I think the word means?

To verify the preliminary determination of the meaning of the word or phrase based on context, consider the following questions:

✓ Does the definition I inferred make sense in the context of the sentence?

✓ Which of the dictionary's definitions makes sense in the context of the sentence?

Skill: Context Clues

Reread paragraph 4 of "Letter to His Daughter." Then, using the Checklist on the previous page, answer the multiple-choice questions below.

YOUR TURN

1. This question has two parts. First, answer Part A. Then, answer Part B.

Part A: What does the word **frank** at the beginning of the passage mean based on the context provided in paragraph 4?

- A. humble
- B. careful
- C. irritated
- D. open

Part B: Which piece of evidence BEST supports your answer to Part A?

- A. "You will meet, of course, curious little annoyances."
- B. "But that simply is of no importance and will soon be forgotten."
- C. ". . . the ability to do, the will to **conquer**, the determination to understand and know. . . "
- D. "Make yourself do unpleasant things, so as to gain the upper hand of your soul."

Close Read

Reread "Letter to His Daughter." As you reread, complete the Skills Focus questions below. Then use your answers and annotations from the questions to help you complete the Write activity.

SKILLS FOCUS

1. In paragraph 4, W.E.B. Du Bois says to his daughter, "Take the cold bath bravely. Enter into the spirit of your big bed-room." Highlight the figurative language and the surrounding sentences that provide context. Explain what you think Du Bois means based on the context.

2. At the end of paragraph 4, Du Bois tells Yolande, "Take yourself in hand and master yourself. Make yourself do unpleasant things, so as to gain the upper hand of your soul." Highlight the figurative language and explain what you think he is asking Yolande to do.

3. Read the following dictionary entry:

   smartness
   smart•ness \'smɑːtnəs\

   noun

   1. the quality of being intelligent
   2. the quality of being quick
   3. the quality of being new and attractive

   Which definition most closely matches the meaning of **smartness** as it is used in paragraph 2? Write the appropriate definition of smartness here and explain how you figured out the correct meaning.

4. Use context clues to determine what the author means when he writes "curious little annoyances."

5. Think about the unit's Essential Question: "Who are you meant to be?" Although Du Bois does not ask Yolande this question, the idea that he wants her to think about her future is implicit in what he says to her. Highlight evidence of this in the letter and explain your reasoning.

WRITE

LITERARY ANALYSIS: In his letter to his daughter, W.E.B. Du Bois often uses figurative language, which allows readers to know more about him. What do his metaphors tell us about who he is and how he thinks people should live? Which of his values or beliefs are evident (AV) in his letter? Be sure to include evidence from the text in your response.

The Story Behind the Bus

INFORMATIONAL TEXT
The Henry Ford® Museum
2002

Introduction

The Henry Ford® museum houses a large collection of items of historical significance, including John F. Kennedy's presidential limousine, Abraham Lincoln's seat from Ford's Theatre, and the bus on which civil rights activist Rosa Parks took her famous stand against segregation. This excerpt from the museum's website offers background information on Rosa Parks and the circumstances surrounding her December 1955 arrest in Montgomery, Alabama.

"When I made that decision," she said later, "I knew that I had the strength of my ancestors with me."

NOTES

1 On December 1, 1955, Rosa Parks, a 42-year-old African American woman who worked as a seamstress, boarded this Montgomery City bus to go home from work. On this bus on that day, Rosa Parks initiated a new era in the American quest for freedom and equality.

2 She sat near the middle of the bus, just behind the 10 seats reserved for whites. Soon all of the seats in the bus were filled. When a white man entered the bus, the driver (following the standard practice of **segregation**) insisted that all four blacks sitting just behind the white section give up their seats so that the man could sit there. Mrs. Parks, who was an active member of the local NAACP[1], quietly refused to give up her seat.

3 Her action was spontaneous and not premeditated, although her previous civil rights involvement and strong sense of justice were obvious influences. "When I made that decision," she said later, "I knew that I had the strength of my ancestors with me."

4 She was arrested and convicted of violating the laws of segregation, known as "Jim Crow laws." Mrs. Parks appealed her conviction and thus formally challenged the legality of segregation.

5 At the same time, local civil rights activists initiated a boycott of the Montgomery bus system. In cities across the South, segregated bus companies were daily reminders of the **inequities** of American society. Since African Americans made up about 75 percent of the riders in Montgomery, the boycott posed a serious economic threat to the company and a social threat to white rule in the city.

6 A group named the Montgomery Improvement Association, composed of local activists and ministers, organized the boycott. As their leader, they chose a young Baptist minister who was new to Montgomery: Martin Luther King, Jr. Sparked by Mrs. Parks's action, the boycott lasted 381 days, into December 1956 when the U.S. Supreme Court ruled that the segregation law

1. **NAACP** the National Association for the Advancement of Colored People (NAACP) is a United States civil rights organization dedicated to advancing justice for African Americans

was **unconstitutional** and the Montgomery buses were **integrated**. The Montgomery Bus Boycott was the beginning of a revolutionary era of non-violent mass protests in support of civil rights in the United States.

7 It was not just an accident that the civil rights movement began on a city bus. In a famous 1896 case involving a black man on a train, *Plessy v. Ferguson*, the U.S. Supreme Court enunciated the "separate but equal" rationale for Jim Crow. Of course, facilities and treatment were never equal.

8 Under Jim Crow customs and laws, it was relatively easy to separate the races in every area of life except transportation. Bus and train companies couldn't afford separate cars and so blacks and whites had to occupy the same space.

9 Thus, transportation was one the most **volatile** arenas for race relations in the South. Mrs. Parks remembers going to elementary school in Pine Level, Alabama, where buses took white kids to the new school but black kids had to walk to their school.

10 "I'd see the bus pass every day," she said. "But to me, that was a way of life; we had no choice but to accept what was the custom. *The bus was among the first ways I realized there was a black world and a white world*" (emphasis added).

11 Montgomery's Jim Crow customs were particularly harsh and gave bus drivers great latitude in making decisions on where people could sit. The law even gave bus drivers the authority to carry guns to enforce their edicts. Mrs. Parks' attorney Fred Gray remembered, "Virtually every African-American person in Montgomery had some negative experience with the buses. But we had no choice. We had to use the buses for transportation."

12 Civil rights advocates had outlawed Jim Crow in interstate train travel, and blacks in several Southern cities attacked the practice of segregated bus systems. There had been a bus boycott in Baton Rouge, Louisiana, in 1953, but black leaders compromised before making real gains. Joann Robinson, a black university professor and activist in Montgomery, had suggested the idea of a bus boycott months before the Parks arrest.

13 Two other women had been arrested on buses in Montgomery before Parks and were considered by black leaders as potential clients for challenging the law. However, both were rejected because black leaders felt they would not gain white support. When she heard that the well-respected Rosa Parks had been arrested, one Montgomery African American woman exclaimed, "They've messed with the wrong one now."

14 In the South, city buses were lightning rods for civil rights activists. It took someone with the courage and character of Rosa Parks to strike with lightning. And it required the commitment of the entire African American community to fan the flames ignited by that lightning into the fires of the civil rights revolution.

WRITE

PERSONAL RESPONSE: When have you calmly or peacefully stood up for something that is important to you or that you believe in? Write about this experience after reflecting on the information in "The Story Behind the Bus." Before you begin, ask yourself, How did Rosa Parks demonstrate her belief? Support your response with evidence from the text.

Rosa

POETRY
Rita Dove
1986

Introduction

studysync tv

Rita Dove (b. 1952) is a highly regarded African American poet and author who won the 1987 Pulitzer Prize for Poetry. Dove's poetic works explore a variety of topics, including historical and political events, and she is known for capturing complex emotions succinctly. Her poem "Rosa" is a tribute to Rosa Parks, the activist who helped end segregation by quietly refusing to leave her seat on the bus.

"Doing nothing was the doing"

NOTES

How she sat there,
the time right inside a place
so wrong it was ready.

That **trim** name with
its dream of a bench
to rest on. Her **sensible** coat.

Doing nothing was the doing:
the clean flame of her gaze
carved by a camera flash.

How she stood up
when they bent down to **retrieve**
her purse. That **courtesy**.

WRITE

PERSONAL RESPONSE: Who is someone you admire? Write a poem about this person imitating Rita Dove's approach in "Rosa." Before you begin, consider how the speaker in the poem shows admiration for Rosa Parks. Include details to make your reasons for admiring this person clear.

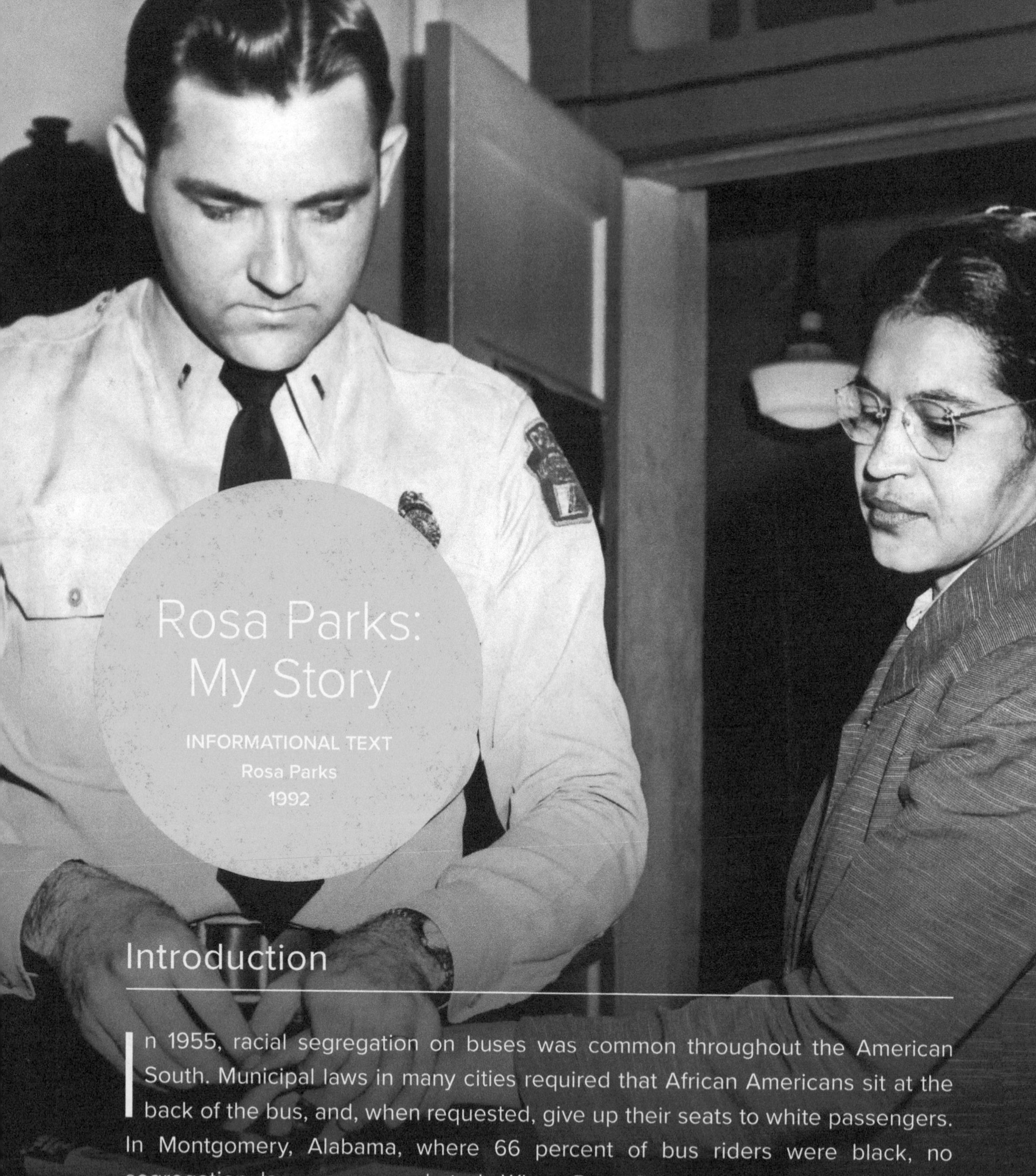

Rosa Parks: My Story

INFORMATIONAL TEXT
Rosa Parks
1992

Introduction

In 1955, racial segregation on buses was common throughout the American South. Municipal laws in many cities required that African Americans sit at the back of the bus, and, when requested, give up their seats to white passengers. In Montgomery, Alabama, where 66 percent of bus riders were black, no segregation law was more hated. When Rosa Parks challenged the law on December 1 and refused an order to give up her seat, her arrest sparked a year-long bus boycott that left the Montgomery public transit system financially crippled. Ms. Parks describes the simple act of civil disobedience that changed history.

"No, the only tired I was, was tired of giving in."

Excerpt from Chapter 8: "You're Under Arrest"

1 When I got off from work that evening of December 1, I went to Court Square as usual to catch the Cleveland Avenue bus home. I didn't look to see who was driving when I got on, and by the time I recognized him, I had already paid my fare[1]. It was the same driver who had put me off the bus back in 1943, twelve years earlier. He was still tall and heavy, with red, rough-looking skin. And he was still mean-looking. I didn't know if he had been on that route before—they switched the drivers around sometimes. I do know that most of the time if I saw him on a bus, I wouldn't get on it.

2 I saw a vacant seat in the middle section of the bus and took it. I didn't even question why there was a vacant seat even though there were quite a few people standing in the back. If I had thought about it at all, I would probably have figured maybe someone saw me get on and did not take the seat but left it vacant for me. There was a man sitting next to the window and two women across the aisle.

3 The next stop was the Empire Theater, and some whites got on. They filled up the white seats, and one man was left standing. The driver looked back and noticed the man standing. Then he looked back at us. He said, "Let me have those front seats," because they were the front seats of the black section. Didn't anybody move. We just sat right where we were, the four of us. Then he spoke a second time: "Y'all better make it light on yourselves and let me have those seats."

4 The man in the window seat next to me stood up, and I moved to let him pass by me, and then I looked across the aisle and saw that the two women were also standing. I moved over to the window seat. I could not see how standing up was going to "make it light" for me. The more we gave in and **complied**, the worse they treated us.

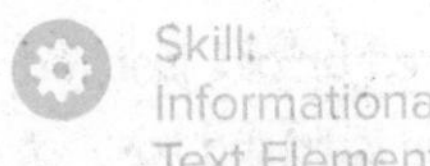

Skill: Informational Text Elements

Parks begins this section of text with the specific date and location where this important event took place. Then, she identifies a key individual and provides some details about him.

Skill: Connotation and Denotation

The denotation of "complied" is "did what was requested"; however, the word is often associated negatively. Here Parks associates "complied" with giving in, and with "the worse they treated us." The connotations suggest that Parks views compliance as a bad choice.

1. **fare** money paid to use public transportation

NOTES

Skill: Informational Text Elements

Here Parks shares a personal anecdote about her grandfather. Then she sets the record straight and explains that she was not tired or old, just fed up. She is trying to explain the true motivation behind her action.

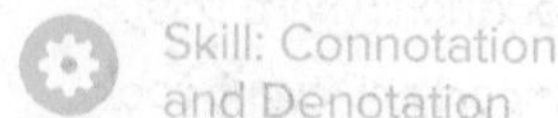

Skill: Connotation and Denotation

Again, Parks has chosen a word with strong negative connotations to emphasize the danger of her situation. The use of the term manhandled adds a sinister or dangerous tone: she is saying that the police could treat her roughly or even beat her.

5 I thought back to the time when I used to sit up all night and didn't sleep, and my grandfather would have his gun right by the fireplace, or if he had his one-horse wagon going anywhere, he always had his gun in the back of the wagon. People always say that I didn't give up my seat because I was tired, but that isn't true. I was not tired physically, or no more tired than I usually was at the end of a working day. I was not old, although some people have an image of me as being old then. I was forty-two. No, the only tired I was, was tired of giving in.

6 The driver of the bus saw me still sitting there, and he asked was I going to stand up. I said, "No." He said, "Well, I'm going to have you arrested." Then I said, "You may do that." These were the only words we said to each other. I didn't even know his name, which was James Blake, until we were in court together. He got out of the bus and stayed outside for a few minutes, waiting for the police.

7 As I sat there, I tried not to think about what might happen. I knew that anything was possible. I could be manhandled or beaten. I could be arrested. People have asked me if it **occurred** to me then that I could be the test case the NAACP had been looking for. I did not think about that at all. In fact if I had let myself think too deeply about what might happen to me, I might have gotten off the bus. But I chose to remain.

8 Meanwhile there were people getting off the bus and asking for transfers, so that began to loosen up the crowd, especially in the back of the bus. Not everyone got off, but everybody was very quiet. What conversation there was, was in low tones; no one was talking out loud. It would have been quite interesting to have seen the whole bus empty out. Or if the other three had stayed where they were, because if they'd had to arrest four of us instead of one, then that would have given me a little support. But it didn't matter. I never thought hard of them at all and never even **bothered** to criticize them.

9 Eventually two policemen came. They got on the bus, and one of them asked me why I didn't stand up. I asked him, "Why do you all push us around?" He said to me, and I quote him exactly, "I don't know, but the law is the law and you're under arrest." One policeman picked up my purse, and the second one picked up my shopping bag and escorted me to the squad car. In the squad car they returned my personal belongings to me. They did not put their hands on me or force me into the car. After I was seated in the car, they went back to the driver and asked him if he wanted to swear out a warrant. He answered that he would finish his route and then come straight back to swear out the warrant. I was only in custody, not legally arrested, until the warrant was signed.

NOTES

10 As they were driving me to the city desk, at City Hall, near Court Street, one of them asked me again, "Why didn't you stand up when the driver spoke to you?" I did not answer. I remained silent all the way to City Hall.

11 As we entered the building, I asked if I could have a drink of water, because my throat was real dry. There was a fountain, and I was standing right next to it. One of the policemen said yes, but by the time I bent down to drink, another policeman said, "No, you can't drink no water. You have to wait until you get to the jail." So I was **denied** the chance to drink a sip of water. I was not going to do anything but wet my throat. I wasn't going to drink a whole lot of water, even though I was quite thirsty. That made me angry, but I did not respond.

12 At the city desk they filled out the necessary forms as I answered questions such as what my name was and where I lived. I asked if I could make a telephone call and they said, "No." Since that was my first arrest, I didn't know if that was more **discrimination** because I was black or if it was standard practice. But it seemed to me to be more discrimination. Then they escorted me back to the squad car, and we went to the city jail on North Ripley Street.

13 I wasn't frightened at the jail. I was more resigned than anything else. I don't recall being real angry, not enough to have an argument. I was just prepared to accept whatever I had to face. I asked again if I could make a telephone call. I was ignored.

14 They told me to put my purse on the counter and to empty my pockets of personal items. The only thing I had in my pocket was a tissue. I took that out. They didn't search me or handcuff me.

15 I was then taken to an area where I was fingerprinted and where mug shots were taken. A white matron[2] came to escort me to my jail cell, and I asked again if I might use the telephone. She told me that she would find out.

16 She took me up a flight of stairs (the cells were on the second level), through a door covered with iron mesh, and along a dimly lighted corridor. She placed me in an empty dark cell and slammed the door closed. She walked a few steps away, but then she turned around and came back. She said, "There are two girls around the other side, and if you want to go over there with them instead of being in a cell by yourself, I will take you over there."

Excerpted from *Rosa Parks: My Story* by Rosa Parks, published by Puffin Books.

2. **matron** a woman serving as a guard, warden, or attendant for women or girls, as in a prison

First Read

Read *Rosa Parks: My Story*. After you read, complete the Think Questions below.

THINK QUESTIONS

1. Refer to one or more details in the text to explain how Rosa's previous interaction with the bus driver might have contributed to her actions on December 1.

2. Use details from the text to explain other factors Parks believes contributed to her actions on December 1, 1955. What do other people seem to think contributed? Does Parks agree?

3. How do the law enforcement officials behave in expected and unexpected ways during Rosa's arrest? Support your answer with textual evidence.

4. Use context to determine the meaning of the word **manhandled** as it is used in *Rosa Parks: My Story*. Write your definition of *manhandled* here and tell how you got it.

5. The Latin word *discriminare* means "to separate." Use this knowledge, along with the context clues provided in the passage, to determine the meaning of **discrimination**. Write your definition of *discrimination* here and explain how you figured it out.

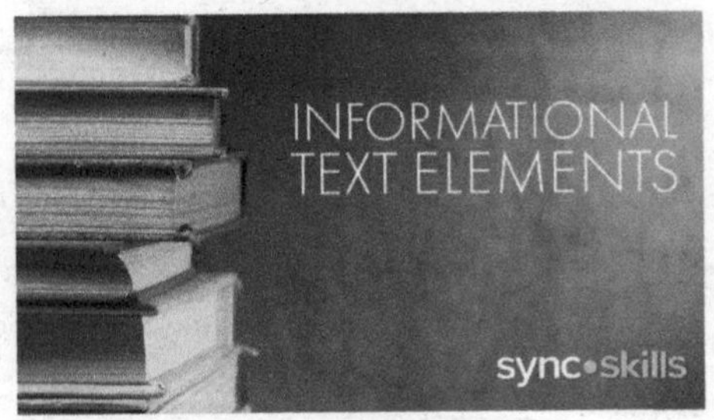

Skill: Informational Text Elements

Use the Checklist to analyze Informational Text Elements in *Rosa Parks: My Story*. Refer to the sample student annotations about Informational Text Elements in the text.

••• CHECKLIST FOR INFORMATIONAL TEXT ELEMENTS

In order to identify a key individual, event, or idea in a text, note the following:

- ✓ examples that describe or explain important ideas, events, or individuals in the text
- ✓ anecdotes in the text. An anecdote is a personal story an author passes on to readers
- ✓ how a key individual, event, or idea is introduced or illustrated
- ✓ other features, such as charts, maps, sidebars, and photos that might provide additional information outside of the main text

To analyze in detail how a key individual, event, or idea is introduced, illustrated, or elaborated in a text, consider the following questions:

- ✓ How does the author introduce or illustrate a key individual, event, or idea?
- ✓ What key details does the author include to describe or elaborate on important information in the text?
- ✓ Does the author include any anecdotes? What do they add to the text?
- ✓ What other features, if any, help readers to analyze the events, ideas, or individuals in the text?

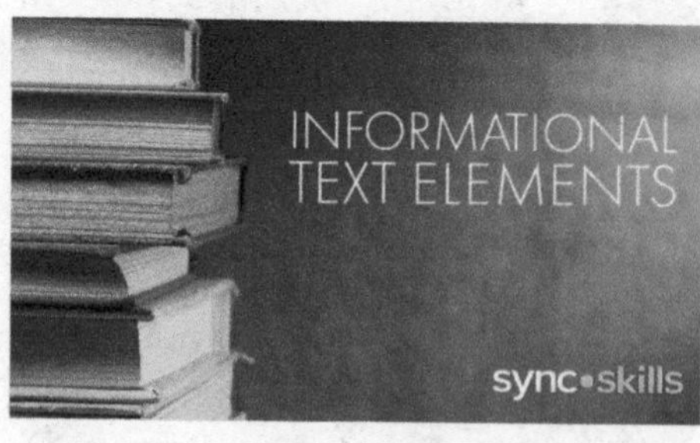

Skill: Informational Text Elements

Reread paragraphs 3 and 4 from *Rosa Parks: My Story*. Then, using the Checklist on the previous page, answer the multiple-choice questions below.

YOUR TURN

1. Which sentence from paragraph 3 is an example of supporting evidence from Parks's autobiography?

   - O A. Then he spoke a second time: "Y'all better make it light on yourselves and let me have those seats."
   - O B. The driver looked back and noticed the man standing.
   - O C. Then he looked back at us.
   - O D. Didn't anybody move.

2. Which sentence from paragraph 4 is a pertinent example from Parks's autobiography?

   - O A. The man in the window seat next to me stood up, and I moved to let him pass by me, and then I looked across the aisle and saw that the two women were also standing.
   - O B. I moved over to the window seat.
   - O C. I could not see how standing up was going to "make it light" for me.
   - O D. The more we gave in and **complied,** the worse they treated us.

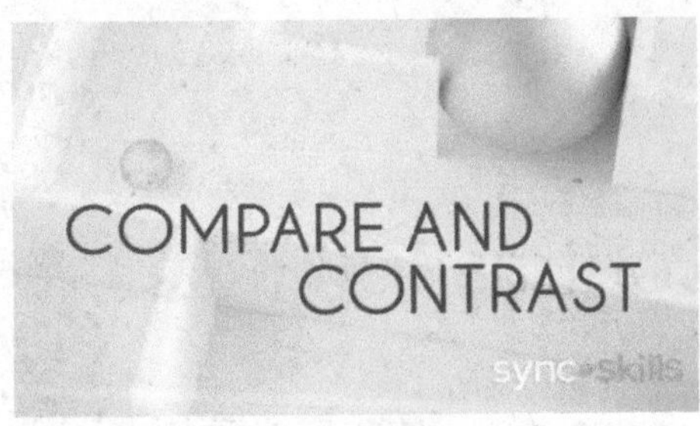

Skill: Compare and Contrast

Use the Checklist to analyze Compare and Contrast in *Rosa Parks: My Story*. Refer to the sample student annotations about Compare and Contrast in the text.

••• CHECKLIST FOR COMPARE AND CONTRAST

In order to determine how to compare and contrast one author's presentation of events with that of another, use the following steps:

- ✓ first, choose two texts with similar subjects or topics, such as an autobiography and a biography of the same person, or a news report of an event and a narrative nonfiction account of the same event
- ✓ next, identify the author's approach to the subject in each genre
- ✓ after, explain how the point of view is different in each text
- ✓ finally, analyze ways in which the texts are similar and different in their presentation of specific events and information
  - whether the nonfiction narrative account contains dialogue that may not have been spoken, or may have been altered in some way
  - what the author of an autobiography might know that a biographer might never be able to uncover or research

To compare and contrast one author's presentation of events with that of another, consider the following questions:

- ✓ How does the author approach each topic or subject?
- ✓ What are the similarities and differences in the presentation of events in each text?

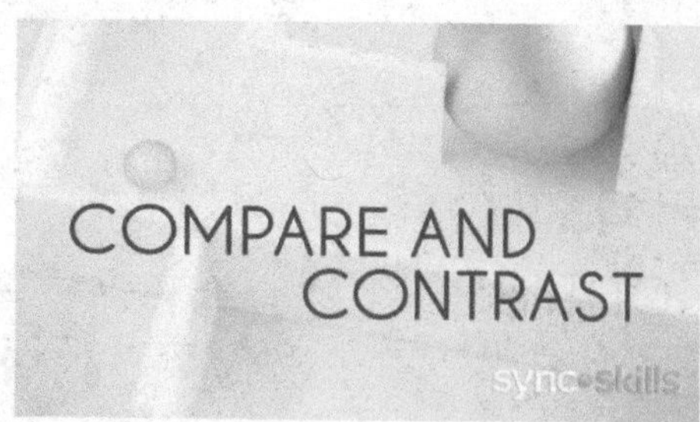

Skill: Compare and Contrast

Drag and drop textual evidence from "The Story Behind the Bus" and *Rosa Parks: My Story* that contrasts the author's presentation of information regarding why Rosa Parks refused to give up her seat in each text.

YOUR TURN

"The Story Behind the Bus"	*Rosa Parks: My Story*
Her action was spontaneous and not premeditated, although her previous civil rights involvement and strong sense of justice were obvious influences.	"People always say that I didn't give up my seat because I was tired, but that isn't true . . . No, the only tired I was, was tired of giving in."

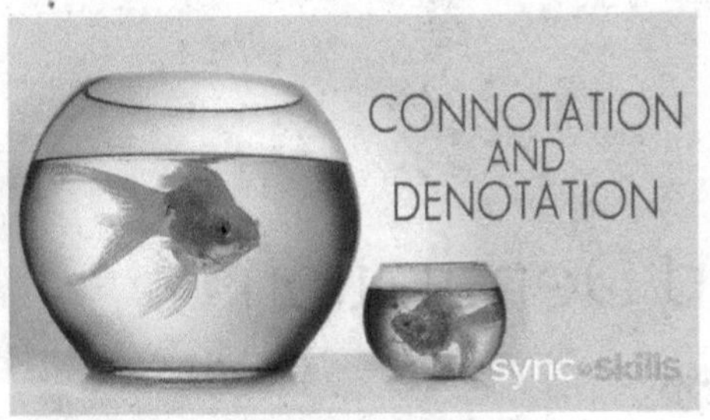

Skill: Connotation and Denotation

Use the Checklist to analyze Connotation and Denotation in *Rosa Parks: My Story*. Refer to the sample student annotations about Connotation and Denotation in the text.

••• CHECKLIST FOR CONNOTATION AND DENOTATION

In order to identify the denotative meanings of words and phrases, use the following steps:

- ✓ first, note unfamiliar words and phrases; key words used to describe important individuals, events, or ideas; or words that inspire an emotional reaction
- ✓ next, verify the denotative meaning of words by consulting a reference work such as a dictionary, glossary, or thesaurus

To better understand the meaning of words and phrases as they are used in a text, including connotative meanings, ask the following questions:

- ✓ What is the genre or subject of the text? How does that affect the possible meaning of a word or phrase?
- ✓ Does the word create a positive, negative, or neutral emotion?
- ✓ What synonyms or alternative phrasing help you describe the connotative meaning of the word?

To determine the meaning of words and phrases as they are used in a text, including connotative meanings, ask the following questions:

- ✓ What is the meaning of the word or phrase? What is the connotation as well as the denotation?
- ✓ If I substitute a synonym based on denotation, is the meaning the same? How does it change the meaning of the text?

Skill: Connotation and Denotation

Reread paragraph 12 of *Rosa Parks: My Story*. Then, using the Checklist on the previous page, answer the multiple-choice questions below.

YOUR TURN

1. This question has two parts. First, answer Part A. Then, answer Part B.

Part A Which of the following is most likely the intended connotation of *discrimination*?

- A. negative—the word suggests confusion and lack of information
- B. neither positive nor negative—the word suggests a separate kind of treatment that is no worse or better.
- C. negative—the word suggests racism and unfair treatment.
- D. positive—the word suggests that Parks was being treated better than others

Part B Which phrase from the passage best supports your answer in Part A?

- A. "was my first arrest"
- B. "because I was black"
- C. "it was standard practice"
- D. "filled out the necessary forms"

Close Read

Reread *Rosa Parks: My Story*. As you reread, complete the Skills Focus questions below. Then use your answers and annotations from the questions to help you complete the Write activity.

SKILLS FOCUS

1. Highlight textual evidence that helps you identify Rosa Parks's purpose for writing her autobiography and the main message for her audience. Explain why Parks wrote *Rosa Parks: My Story* and what she wants her audience to understand about her life.

2. The primary purpose of an autobiography is to detail the events of an individual's life, and these events must be supported with evidence and pertinent examples. In *My Story*, Rosa Parks uses these elements to tell her story. Analyze how Parks uses supporting evidence and pertinent examples to support her purpose for writing.

3. In *Rosa Parks: My Story*, the author uses several words whose connotations are specific to her story. Select a word from the text, identify its denotation, and then explain its connotation as used in the context.

4. In the poem "Rosa," Rita Dove expresses the idea that "Doing nothing was the doing." Identify evidence in the autobiography that supports this claim and explain your reasoning.

5. Identify evidence in *Rosa Parks: My Story* that Parks was true to herself and how her actions shaped who she was meant to be.

WRITE

COMPARATIVE: Rosa Parks, Rita Dove, and the author of "The Story Behind the Bus" all have a story to share about upsetting the balance of power. How does each author introduce, illustrate, or elaborate this idea of power? How are their arguments about power similar and different? In your response, remember to make connections to ideas in the previous (AV) texts that you've read.

Eleanor Roosevelt: A Life of Discovery

INFORMATIONAL TEXT
Russell Freedman
1993

Introduction

studysync

Initially reluctant to be a president's wife, "poor little rich girl" Eleanor Roosevelt (1884–1962) rose to the challenge of being in the national spotlight. Bright, energetic, and courageous, she became the most celebrated and admired first lady the White House had ever known. As an invaluable researcher for her husband during the years of the Great Depression, and later a representative of the United Nations, Eleanor raised the bar of possibilities for all first ladies who followed her.

"Americans had never seen a First Lady like her. . ."

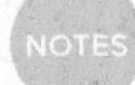

Excerpt from Chapter One: First Lady

1 Eleanor Roosevelt never wanted to be a president's wife. When her husband Franklin won his **campaign** for the presidency in 1932, she felt deeply troubled. She dreaded the prospect of living in the White House.

2 Proud of her accomplishments as a teacher, a writer, and a political power in her own right, she feared that she would have to give up her hard-won independence in Washington. As First Lady, she would have no life of her own. Like other presidential wives before her, she would be assigned the traditional role of official White House hostess, with little to do but greet guests at receptions and preside over formal state dinners.

3 "From the personal standpoint, I did not want my husband to be president," she later confessed. "It was pure selfishness on my part, and I never mentioned my feelings on the subject to him."

4 Mrs. Roosevelt did her duty. During her years in the White House, the executive mansion[1] bustled with visitors at teas, receptions, and dinners. At the same time, however, she cast her fears aside and seized the opportunity to transform the role of America's First Lady. Encouraged by her friends, she became the first wife of a president to have a public life and career.

5 Americans had never seen a First Lady like her. She was the first to open the White House door to reporters and hold on-the-record[2] press conferences[3], the first to drive her own car, to travel by plane, and to make many official trips by herself. "My missus goes where she wants to!" the president boasted.

1. **executive mansion** the White House is considered the headquarters of the executive branch of the U.S. government
2. **on-the-record** making one's statements official or public
3. **press conferences** interviews granted to journalists to communicate information and answer questions

6 She was the first president's wife to earn her own money by writing, lecturing, and broadcasting. Her earnings usually topped the president's salary. She gave most of the money to charity.

7 When she insisted on her right to take drives by herself, without a chauffeur or a police escort, the Secret Service, worried about her safety, gave her a pistol and begged her to carry it with her. "I [took] it and learned how to use it," she told readers of her popular newspaper column. "I do not mean by this that I am an expert shot. I only wish I were . . . . My opportunities for shooting have been far and few between, but if the necessity arose, I do know how to use a pistol."

8 She had come a long way since her days as an obedient society matron[4], and, before then, a **timid** child who was "always afraid of something." By her own account, she had been an "ugly duckling" whose mother told her, "You have no looks, so see to it that you have manners." Before she was ten, both of her unhappy parents were dead. She grew up in a time and place where a woman's life was ruled by her husband's interests and needs, and dominated by the domestic duties of wife and mother. "It was not until I reached middle age," she wrote, "that I had the courage to develop interests of my own, outside of my duties to my family."

9 Eleanor Roosevelt lived in the White House during the Great Depression and the Second World War. In her endless travels through America, she served as a fact-finder and trouble-shooter for her husband and an impassioned publicist for her own views about social justice and world peace. She wanted people to feel that their government cared about them. After Franklin Roosevelt's death, she became a major force at the United Nations, where her efforts on behalf of human rights earned her the title, First Lady of the World.

10 People meeting her for the first time often were startled by how "unjustly" the camera treated her. Photographs had not prepared them for her warmth and dignity and **poise**. An unusually tall woman, she moved with the grace of an athlete, and when she walked into a room, the air seemed charged with her **vibrancy**. "No one seeing her could fail to be moved," said her friend Martha Gellhorn. "She gave off light, I cannot explain it better."

11 For thirty years from the time she entered the White House until her death in 1962, Eleanor Roosevelt was the most famous and at times the most **influential** woman in the world. And yet those who knew her best were most impressed by her simplicity, by her total lack of self-importance.

4. **matron** a dignified married woman

12 "About the only value the story of my life may have," she wrote, "is to show that one can, even without any particular gifts, overcome obstacles that seem insurmountable if one is willing to face the fact that they must be overcome; that, in spite of timidity and fear, in spite of a lack of special talents, one can find a way to live widely and fully."

Excerpted from *Eleanor Roosevelt: A Life of Discovery* by Russell Freedman, published by Clarion Books.

WRITE

PERSONAL RESPONSE: Eleanor Roosevelt did not wish to become First Lady of the United States. Yet she was able to overcome her fear to become one of the most beloved First Ladies in history. Consider how Eleanor's life might relate to your own. Is there a task or dream you would like to achieve? How can you, like Eleanor, overcome any fears you might have in order to achieve success? In your response, write about the goal or dream you have been afraid to achieve. Then, explain what strategy you can use, like Eleanor, to overcome that fear.

Brave

FICTION

Svetlana Chmakova

2017

Introduction

Svetlana Chmakova (b. 1979), a Russian and Canadian comic artist, published *Brave* as a sequel to her graphic novel, *Awkward*. Brave follows Jensen, a middle school boy who dreams of saving the world. Jensen soon finds that saving the world and following his dreams aren't as easy as they sound, however, and he must learn to be brave as he faces challenges along the way.

"I may be just a regular kid at regular Berrybrook Middle School . . . but I am going to save the world."

NOTES

6

1. **sunspots** dark spots or patches appearing from time to time on the sun's surface, known to cause magnetic disturbances on Earth

NOTES

...THERE ARE MANY ZOMBIE WARNING SIGNS IN MY MATH CLASS...
URGH
I BETTER BE CAREFUL.

...OF COURSE, IT COULD JUST BE THAT THIS IS MATH...

...WITH MR. KRISTOFFER, THE MOST BORING AND EVIL MATH TEACHER IN THE UNIVERSE.
PAY ATTENTION, CLASS, OR IT'S EXTRA HOMEWORK AGAIN FOR EVERYONE!

I HAAAAATE MATH.
BUT MOM SAID I'LL NEED IT FOR WHAT I WANT TO BE—

AN ASTRONAUT AT NASA!

7

NOTES

I CAN'T WAIT TO BE A REAL ASTRONAUT.
I'M GOING TO BEAT THE LONGEST SPACE WALK RECORD...
WHEE!
...AND WHEN I GO TO MARS, I'M GONNA DISCOVER AN ANCIENT CIVILIZATION.
earth
DUST
DUST
alien statue
...JENSEN.
JENSEN...?
JENSEN!!
...FOR THE LAST TIME, WHAT IS THE CORRECT ANSWER TO THIS PROBLEM?
8

$42 \div \frac{5}{8} = ?$

UH...

UM...

IS...IT...

...67?

68!

...81?

NO, IT MOST CERTAINLY IS NOT!

NOOOO

NO.

!

NO...

THAT'S IT!! EXTRA HOMEWORK FOR EVERYONE!! TWENTY PROBLEMS BY TOMORROW!!

GRRR

THANKS A LOT!

...

WTH, JENSEN?

AGAIN?

I WISH THE ZOMBIE SURVIVAL GUIDE COVERED SITUATIONS LIKE THIS...

9

RRRING
GRUMBLE
stupid jensen.
GLARE
...
...

IT'S OKAY. NEXT CLASS WILL BE BETTER.

IT'S ENGLISH! I REALLY LIKE THE TEACHER, MISS LEE...

...AND I HAVE A FRIEND THERE, PENELOPE TORRES.

WE'RE IN THE ART CLUB TOGETHER.

I JUST NEED TO GET THERE WITHOUT—

!

HEY, FATSO.

WHEN ARE YOU GONNA LEARN FRACTIONS, PEA BRAIN?

IF WE HAVE TO DO **ANY MORE** HOMEWORK BECAUSE OF YOU, I'M GONNA MAKE YOU REGRET IT. GOT THAT?

10

NOTES

I-I...
I'M SORRY...?
SNAP
SNAP
NOT YET. YOU ARE
HEY, WHAT'S GOING ON HERE?
...!

JENNY!!
FOSTER?
YANIC?
IS THERE A PROBLEM?

UH...NO...
WE GOTTA GET TO CLASS.
LATER!
LATER, JENSEN.
BUT HOPEFULLY NEVER!

11

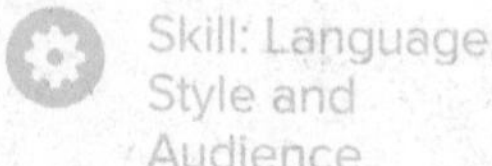

Skill: Language, Style and Audience

In Jensen's daydream he says "I can't wait to be." This language choice shows that he's excited for the future. In the next panel, Jensen's name is in capital letters with multiple exclamation points. His daydream gets interupted, and his attitude changes.

12

NOTES

Skill: Language, Style and Audience

I can see that the other students and the teacher are frustrated because the author included angry and sarcastic words and phrases directed at Jensen. The tone seems very tense.

NOTES

14

2. **running the gauntlet** enduring an intimidating or dangerous task

NOTES

START!
...WITHOUT GETTING EATEN BY THE GAME MONSTERS...
MORE WORK!
GRRR
YOU SUCK!
HSSS
CHOMP
CHOMP
...TO WIN THE PRIZE AT THE END OF THE LEVEL...

NOTES

THE ART CLUB
...WHERE I CAN JUST SIT, DRAW, AND NO ONE EVER BOTHERS ME.
I JUST HAVE TO MAKE IT TO THE END OF THE DAY...
ENGLIS
...OKAY, GUYS, SETTLE DOWN! THIS IS ENGLISH, NOT A TRIP TO THE ZOO!
I'M GOING TO FINISH TAKING ATTENDANCE NOW.
16

NOTES

...PENELOPE TORRES?
HERE!
THAT'S HER! MY FRIEND FROM ART CLUB.

I THINK...SHE'S DRAWING SOMETHING.

STRETCH

JENSEN GRAHAM?
....!
UH, HERE!

JORGE RUIZ?
HERE.
...I'M GONNA SKETCH TOO.

I'VE BEEN ON A BIG SPACESHIP KICK LATELY...
NASA SAYS THEY NEED NEW SHIP DESIGNS, SO I—

17

NOTES

MISS TORRES.
MR. GRAHAM.
PUT THOSE SKETCHES AWAY AND PAY ATTENTION PLEASE.
WE'RE STARTING ON GROUP PRESENTATIONS TODAY.
EVERYONE, PICK YOUR GROUPS NOW!
NO MORE THAN THREE PEOPLE PER GROUP AND NO FEWER THAN TWO, FOR OBVIOUS REASONS.
GROUP OF TWO?
THAT'S ME AND PENELOPE! I'M GONNA ASK...
HEY, PENELOPE! WANNA BE IN OUR GROUP?
!!
YEAH, OKAY!
...
18

First Read

Read the excerpt from the graphic novel *Brave*. After you read, complete the Think Questions below.

THINK QUESTIONS

1. Why does Jensen carry around a book titled "Zombie Survival Guide"? Cite evidence from page 6 to support your response.

2. According to pages 14–16, how does Jensen deal with challenges?

3. Why do the other kids leave Jensen alone when Jenny, Akilah, and Felipe arrive? Cite evidence from the text to support your response.

4. Based on context clues from page 6, determine the meaning of **apocalypse** as it is used in the text. Then confirm your inferred meaning by checking an online or print dictionary.

5. Read the following dictionary entry:

   lurk
   \lərk\
   verb

   1. to remain hidden while waiting to pounce (said of a person or animal)
   2. to be difficult to detect, but still threatening
   3. to read internet message boards without writing on them

   Which definition most closely matches the meaning of *lurk* on page 6 and again on page 6? Write the correct definition of *lurk* here and explain how you figured it out.

Skill: Language, Style, and Audience

Use the Checklist to analyze Language, Style, and Audience in *Brave*. Refer to the sample student annotations about Language, Style, and Audience in the text.

••• CHECKLIST FOR LANGUAGE, STYLE, AND AUDIENCE

In order to determine an author's style, do the following:

- ✓ identify and define any unfamiliar words or phrases
- ✓ use context, including the meaning of surrounding words and phrases
- ✓ note possible reactions to the author's word choice
- ✓ examine your reaction to the author's word choice, and how the author's word choice affected your reaction

To analyze the impact of specific word choice on meaning and tone, ask the following questions:

- ✓ How did your understanding of the language change during your analysis?
- ✓ What stylistic choices can you identify in the text? How does the style influence your understanding of the language?
- ✓ How could different audiences interpret this language? What different possible emotional responses can you list?
- ✓ How does the writer's choice of words create a specific tone in the text?

Skill: Language, Style, and Audience

Reread pages 10 and 11 of *Brave*. Then, using the Checklist on the previous page, answer the multiple-choice questions below.

YOUR TURN

1. This question has two parts. First, answer Part A. Then, answer Part B.

Part A What does the word choice on these pages tell you about Jensen's character and the tone of the story?

- A. They show that Jensen is always sad and thinks the worst will happen.
- B. They show that Jensen doesn't have many challenges.
- C. They show that even though Jensen is often bullied, he remains optimistic.
- D. They show that Jensen doesn't care what other students think of him and that bullies don't bother him.

Part B Which of the following details DOES NOT support your response to Part A?

- A. "We're in the art club together."
- B. "It's okay. Next class will be better."
- C. "I just need to get there without—"
- D. "Later! But hopefully never!"

Close Read

Reread *Brave*. As you reread, complete the Skills Focus questions below. Then use your answers and annotations from the questions to help you complete the Write activity.

SKILLS FOCUS

1. Identify panels in *Brave* where the illustrations and speech bubbles work together to help you understand how Jensen views life. Explain how these visuals enhance your understanding of Jensen.

2. Identify panels in *Brave* where the style of the speech bubbles, used for characters other than Jensen, allows the audience to interpret the text's meaning. Explain what the style of the speech bubbles adds to your understanding.

3. Eleanor Roosevelt described herself as a shy 'ugly duckling' who only later in life got the courage to be herself. Highlight evidence that suggests how Jensen might relate to Roosevelt's childhood. Explain your reasoning.

4. Identify two unknown words from the passage and explain how to use word patterns and relationships to determine their meanings.

5. Identify panels in *Brave* that help you predict how Jensen might answer the Essential Question: "Who are you meant to be?" Explain how you think he might answer based on the evidence.

WRITE

DISCUSSION: What does it mean to be true to yourself? In a discussion with your peers, imagine how Jensen and Eleanor Roosevelt would respond to this question. What would they say? What advice would they offer? How might they agree or disagree? Cite examples of specific word choices and tone that express how they are true to themselves.

I Never Had It Made: An Autobiography of Jackie Robinson

INFORMATIONAL TEXT

Jackie Robinson

1972

Introduction

In 1947, Jackie Robinson (1919–1972), a talented baseball player and man of great character, made history as the first African American baseball player to "break the color barrier" and play in modern Major League Baseball. In this excerpt from his autobiography, Robinson reflects back on his experience and its impact on American society.

"... a sport can't be called national if blacks are barred from it."

From the Preface: Today
Jackie Robinson

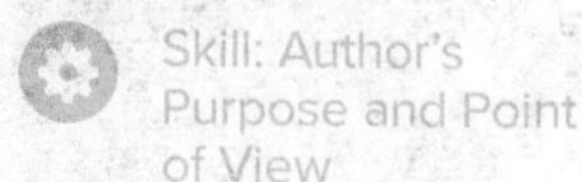

Skill: Author's Purpose and Point of View

I think Robinson's purpose must be to inform the reader because he gives details about the time, place, and the importance he gives to a special day in his life.

1 I guess if I could choose one of the most important moments in my life, I would go back to 1947, in the Yankee Stadium in New York City. **It** was the opening day of the world series and I was for the first time playing in the series as a member of the Brooklyn Dodgers team. It was a history-making day. It would be the first time that a black man would be allowed to **participate** in a world series. I had become the first black player in the major leagues.

2 I was proud of that and yet I was uneasy. I was proud to be in the hurricane eye[1] of a significant breakthrough and to be used to prove that a sport can't be called national if blacks are barred from it. Branch Rickey, the president of the Brooklyn Dodgers, had rudely awakened America. He was a man with high ideals, and he was also a shrewd businessman. Mr. Rickey had shocked some of his fellow baseball tycoons and angered others by deciding to smash the unwritten law that kept blacks out of the big leagues. He had chosen me as the person to lead the way.

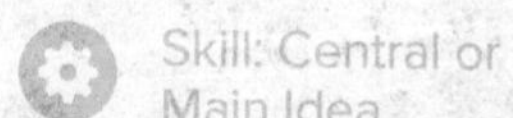

Skill: Central or Main Idea

I can see that Jackie Robinson endured hard times in baseball because of his race. I think this is the central idea of the paragraph.

These details directly support the idea that Robinson dealt with hate and went through hard times.

3 It hadn't been easy. Some of my own teammates refused to accept me because I was black. I had been forced to live with snubs and rebuffs and rejections. Within the club, Mr. Rickey had put down rebellion by letting my teammates know that anyone who didn't want to accept me could leave. But the problems within the Dodgers club had been minor compared to the opposition outside. It hadn't been that easy to fight the resentment expressed by players on other teams, by the team owners, or by **bigoted** fans screaming "n-----." The hate mail piled up. There were threats against me and my family and even out-and-out attempts at physical harm to me.

4 Some things counterbalanced this ugliness. Black people supported me with total loyalty. They supported me morally: they came to sit in a **hostile** audience in unprecedented numbers to make the turnstiles[2] hum as they never had

1. **hurricane eye** the center of a storm
2. **turnstiles** mechanical gates of revolving horizontal arms allowing only one person at a time to pass through

before at ballparks all over the nation. Money is America's God, and business people can dig black power if it **coincides** with green power, so these fans were important to the success of Mr. Rickey's "Noble Experiment."

5 Some of the Dodgers who swore they would never play with a black man had a change of mind, when they realized I was a good ballplayer who could be l in their earning a few thousand more dollars in world series money. After the initial resistance to me had been crushed, my teammates started to give me tips in how to improve my game. They hadn't changed because they liked me any better; they had changed because I could help fill their wallets.

6 My fellow Dodgers were not decent out of self-interest alone. There were heartwarming experiences with some teammates; there was Southern-born Pee Wee Reese, who turned into a staunch friend. And there were others.

7 Mr. Rickey stands out as the man who inspired me the most. He will always have my admiration and respect. Critics had said, "Don't you know that your precious Mr. Rickey didn't bring you up out of the black leagues because he loved you? Are you stupid enough not to understand that the Brooklyn club profited hugely because of what your Mr. Rickey did?"

8 Yes, I know that. But I also know what a big gamble he took. A **bond** developed between us that lasted long after I had left the game. In a way I feel I was the son he had lost and he was the father I had lost.

9 There was more than just making money at stake in Mr. Rickey's decision. I learned that his family was afraid that his health was being undermined by the resulting pressures and that they pleaded with him to abandon the plan. His peers and fellow baseball moguls exerted all kinds of influence to get him to change his mind. Some of the press condemned him as a fool and a demagogue[3]. But he didn't give in.

10 In a very real sense, black people helped make the experiment succeed. Many who came to the ball park had not been baseball fans before I began to play in the big leagues. Suppressed and repressed for so many years, they needed a victorious black man as a symbol. It would help them believe in themselves. But black support of the first black man in the majors was a complicated matter. The breakthrough created as much danger as it did hope. It was one thing for me out there on the playing field to be able to keep my cool in the face of insults. But it was another for all those black people sitting in the stands to keep from overreacting when they sensed a racial slur or an unjust decision. . . . I learned from Rachel, who had spent hours in the

Skill: Central or Main Idea

I think Jackie is trying to say that he was accepted by his team after they realized he could help earn them money.

The fact that his teammates were using him further supports the idea that he was mistreated because of his race.

3. **demagogue** a leader who appeals to ignorance and prejudice rather than using rational argument

NOTES

stands, that clergymen and laymen had held meetings in the black community to spread the word. We all knew about the help of the black press. Mr. Rickey and I owed them a great deal.

11 Children from all races came to the stands. The very young seemed to have no hangup at all about my being black. They just wanted me to be good, to deliver, to win. The inspiration of their innocence is amazing. I don't think I'll ever forget the small, shrill voice of a tiny white kid who, in the midst of a racially tense atmosphere during an early game in a Dixie town, cried out, "Attaboy, Jackie." It broke the tension and it made me feel I had to succeed.

12 The black and the young were my cheering squads. But also there were people—neither black nor young—people of all races and faiths and in all parts of the country, people who couldn't care less about my race.

13 Rachel was even more important to my success. I know that every successful man is supposed to say that without his wife he could never have accomplished success. It is gospel in my case. Rachel shared those difficult years that led to this moment and helped me through all the days thereafter. She has been strong, loving, gentle, and brave, never afraid to either criticize or comfort me.

Excerpted from *I Never Had It Made* by Jackie Robinson, published by HarperCollins Publishers

First Read

Read *I Never Had It Made: An Autobiography of Jackie Robinson*. After you read, complete the Think Questions below.

 THINK QUESTIONS

1. Why does Jackie Robinson feel uneasy about the opening day of the World Series? Refer to direct evidence as well as to clues you infer from the text.

2. Use details from the text to write two or three sentences describing the different ways people treated Jackie Robinson.

3. Write two or three sentences exploring who Jackie Robinson credits with contributing to his success and why. Support your answer with textual evidence.

4. Use context to determine the meaning of the word **bigoted** as it is used in paragraph 3. Write your definition here and identify clues that helped you figure out its meaning.

5. Use the context clues provided in the passage to determine the meaning of the word **coincides** as it is used in paragraph 4. Write your definition here and identify clues that helped you figure out its meaning. Then check the meaning in a dictionary.

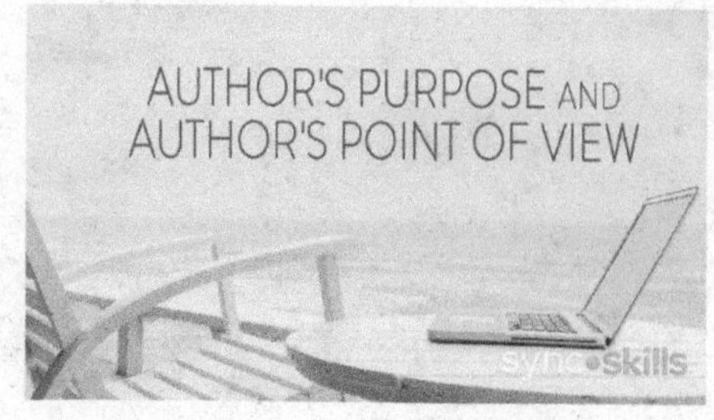

Skill: Author's Purpose and Point of View

Use the Checklist to analyze Author's Purpose and Point of View in *I Never Had It Made: An Autobiography of Jackie Robinson*. Refer to the sample student annotations about Author's Purpose and Point of View in the text.

••• CHECKLIST FOR AUTHOR'S PURPOSE AND POINT OF VIEW

In order to identify author's purpose and point of view, note the following:

- ✓ facts, statistics, and graphic aids as these indicate that the author is writing to inform
- ✓ the author's use of emotional or figurative language, which may indicate that the author is trying to persuade readers or stress an opinion
- ✓ descriptions that present a complicated process in plain language, which may indicate that the author is writing to explain
- ✓ the language the author uses, as figurative and emotional language can be clues to the author's point of view on a subject or topic

To determine the author's purpose and point of view in a text, consider the following questions:

- ✓ How does the author convey, or communicate, information in the text?
- ✓ Does the author use figurative or emotional language? For what purpose does the author use it?
- ✓ Does the author make use of charts, graphs, maps and other graphic aids?

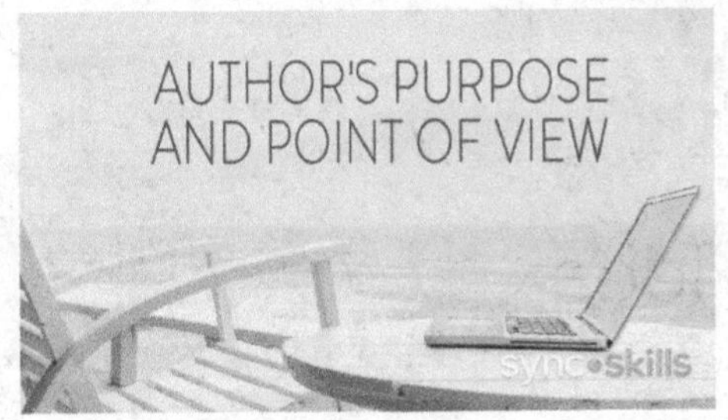

Skill: Author's Purpose and Point of View

Reread paragraphs 9–12 from *I Never Had It Made: An Autobiography of Jackie Robinson*. Then, using the Checklist on the previous page, answer the multiple-choice questions below.

YOUR TURN

1. The author's purpose for including the information about Mr. Rickey in paragraph 9 may have been to explain that —

   - ○ A. Mr. Rickey was not well when he put his plan into action.
   - ○ B. Mr. Rickey stuck with his decisions for many reasons.
   - ○ C. the press easily influenced Mr. Rickey.
   - ○ D. other baseball moguls supported Mr. Rickey's plan.

2. What is one idea the author wants readers to understand from the information in paragraph 10?

   - ○ A. The black press held meetings to support Jackie Robinson.
   - ○ B. Black baseball fans filled the stands when Jackie Robinson played.
   - ○ C. Black people were willing to face possible danger to support Jackie Robinson.
   - ○ D. Black baseball fans helped Jackie Robinson keep his cool on the field.

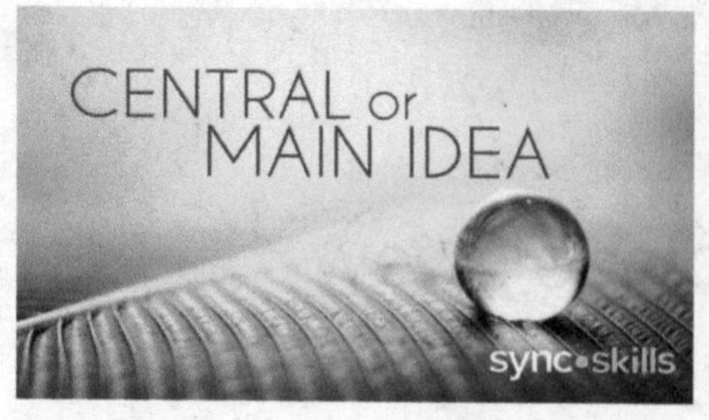

Skill: Central or Main Idea

Use the Checklist to analyze Central or Main Idea in *I Never Had It Made: An Autobiography of Jackie Robinson*. Refer to the sample student annotations about Central or Main Idea in the text.

••• CHECKLIST FOR CENTRAL OR MAIN IDEA

In order to identify a central idea of a text, note the following:

- ✓ the topic or subject of the text
- ✓ the central or main idea, if it is explicitly stated
- ✓ details in the text that convey the theme

To determine a central idea of a text and how it is conveyed through particular details, consider the following questions:

- ✓ What main idea do the details in one or more paragraphs explain or describe?
- ✓ What bigger idea do all the paragraphs support?
- ✓ What is the best way to state the central idea? How might you summarize the text and message?
- ✓ How do particular details in the text convey the central idea?

Skill: Central or Main Idea

Reread paragraphs 9–11 of *I Never Had It Made: An Autobiography of Jackie Robinson*. Then, using the Checklist on the previous page, answer the multiple-choice questions below.

YOUR TURN

1. Which statement best expresses the central idea of paragraph 9?

   ○ A. Mr. Rickey's choice to draft Jackie was risky for both the team and for his own success.
   ○ B. Jackie trusted Mr. Rickey and hoped that his health would not decline because of baseball.
   ○ C. Mr. Rickey wished his peers would understand and support his decision to sign Jackie.
   ○ D. The press and Mr. Rickey's colleagues bashed his decision and ultimately changed his mind.

2. Which statement best expresses the central idea of the whole passage (paragraphs 9–11)?

   ○ A. Jackie Robinson was a talented baseball player who was supported by Mr. Rickey.
   ○ B. Jackie Robinson greatly appreciated the encouragement of his peers while with the Dodgers.
   ○ C. Jackie Robinson relied on Mr. Rickey, his fans, and the black community to flourish.
   ○ D. Jackie Robinson wished that he had more assistance from the white community.

Close Read

Reread *I Never Had It Made: An Autobiography of Jackie Robinson*. As you reread, complete the Skills Focus questions below. Then use your answers and annotations from the questions to help you complete the Write activity.

SKILLS FOCUS

1. Several people and groups affected Jackie Robinson's life in a positive way as he broke the color barrier in baseball. Identify evidence of the effect these people and groups had on Robinson and explain what he wants the reader to understand about their effect on him.

2. How does the cause/effect relationship between the word *counterbalanced* and the examples in paragraph 4 that follow help you determine the meaning of the word? Cite evidence from the paragraph to support your answer.

3. Robinson credits the black community with helping make his entry into the major leagues a success. Identify evidence of the black community's contributions and explain how you would restate the main ideas and the most important details in your own words.

4. What is the central or main idea of paragraph 2 of the text? Cite textual evidence to support your response.

5. Identify evidence that supports the idea that many factors helped Jackie Robinson become who he was meant to be. Explain your reasoning.

WRITE

ARGUMENTATIVE: Jackie Robinson once said, "A life is not important except in the impact it has on other lives." How does the excerpt from his autobiography, *I Never Had It Made: An Autobiography of Jackie Robinson* support this statement? Thinking of this quote, why do you think Robinson chose to write an autobiography? Include evidence from the text as you form your response.

Touching Spirit Bear

FICTION
Ben Mikaelsen
2001

Introduction

Cole Matthews is an angry teenager with a talent for getting into trouble. This time, however, he's facing jail time for brutally beating up a fellow classmate, Peter Driscal. When Cole's parole officer, Garvey, offers him an alternative to prison in a Native American program called Circle Justice, Cole jumps at the opportunity—even though he's skeptical of just about anything and anyone. As part of his rehabilitation, Cole is sent by a Tlingit elder to a remote island in the Alaskan wilderness to think about his mistakes and discover his place in the order of things. Winner of the Nautilus Book Award, *Touching Spirit Bear* is Bolivian-American children's author Ben Mikaelsen's gripping tale about how Cole faces his demons and learns to heal.

"You're part of a much bigger circle. Learn your place or you'll have a rough time."

Chapter 2

1 The heavy load of supplies caused the skiff to wallow through the waves. Cole examined the boxes filled with canned foods, clothes, bedroll, ax, cooking gear, heavy rain gear, rubber boots, and even school work he was supposed to complete. He chuckled. Fat chance he'd ever do any schoolwork.

2 Several weeks earlier, Edwin, the Tlingit[1] elder from Drake, had built a **sparse** one-room wood shelter for Cole on the island. He described the interior as bare except for a small wood stove and a bed—a good place for a soul to think and heal.

3 Cole resented the cabin and all this gear. When his father had agreed to pay all the expenses of banishment, it was just another one of his buyouts. Cole had news for him. This was just a sorry game. He twisted harder at the handcuffs and winced at the pain. He wasn't afraid of pain. He wasn't afraid of anyone or anything. He was only playing along until he could escape. He glanced back at Garvey. The whole Circle Justice thing had been such a joke. Back in Minneapolis, he had been forced to plead guilty and ask the Circle for help changing his life.

4 Asking for help was a simple con job, but he hadn't liked the idea of pleading guilty. "That's like hanging myself," he had complained to Garvey.

5 "You can **withdraw** your guilty plea and go through standard justice any time you want," Garvey said. "But once you go to trial, it's too late for Circle Justice." When Cole hesitated, Garvey added, "I thought you liked being in control, Champ."

6 Cole didn't trust anyone, but what choice did he have? "Okay," he answered **reluctantly.** "But if you're lying, you'll be sorry."

7 Garvey feigned surprise. "Let me get this straight, Champ. You figure if I'm scared of you, you can trust me?" He smiled thinly. "You sure have a lot to learn about trust."

1. **Tlingit** indigenous peoples of the Pacific Northwest

8 "Quit calling me Champ," Cole mumbled. "That's not my name." Then grudgingly he held his tongue. Nobody was going to make him lose his cool. This was a game he planned to win. "So," he asked, "how soon do I start this Circle Justice stuff?"

9 "You can apply, but that doesn't mean you're automatically accepted. First the Circle committee will visit with you. They'll talk to Peter Driscal and his family, your parents, and others to decide if you're serious about wanting change. It might take weeks." Garvey hesitated. "Remember something else. You're wasting everybody's time if you don't truly want to change."

10 Cole nodded obediently, like a little puppy that would follow every rule and jump through any hoop. When he reached the island, that would all come to a screeching stop. Then he would prove to the whole world he was nobody's fool.

11 Cole heard the motor slow and realized that Edwin was guiding the skiff toward a protected bay on the large island ahead. The distant green-black forests were **shrouded** in gray mist. Cole spotted the tiny shelter that had been built for him near the trees, above the shoreline. Black tar paper covered the small wooden structure. Cole spit again at the waves. If these fossils really thought he was going to live in that shack for a whole year, they were nuts.

12 As the skiff[2] scraped the rocks, Garvey jumped out and pulled the boat ashore. Still handcuffed, Cole crawled awkwardly over the bow onto the slippery rocks. Edwin began immediately to unload the supplies.

13 "Why don't you take my handcuffs off and let me help?" Cole asked.

14 Garvey and Edwin ignored his question. One at a time they carried the heavy cardboard boxes up to the shelter and stacked them inside the door. When they finished, Edwin motioned for Cole to follow him up to the mossy bench of ground above the tide line. Cole **moseyed** along slowly, not catching up to Edwin until they reached the trees.

15 Edwin turned to Cole. "Nobody's going to baby-sit you here. If you eat you'll live. If not, you'll die. This land can provide for you or kill you." He pointed into the forest. "Winters are long. Cut plenty of wood or you'll freeze. Keep things dry, because wet kills."

16 "I'm not afraid of dying," Cole boasted.

17 Edwin smiled slightly. "If death stares you straight in the face, believe me, son, you'll get scared." He pointed to a tall plant with snake-like branches. "This

Skill: Setting

The setting is clearly the forest and the way Edwin describes it, it seems that it is potentially deadly. Cole could get really hurt if he isn't careful. I wonder how this will affect Cole in the story

2. **skiff** a shallow open boat with sharp bow and square stern

NOTES

island is covered with Devil's Club. Don't grab it or hundreds of tiny thistles will infect your hands and make them swell up like sausages." Edwin motioned toward the head of the bay, a quarter mile away. "The stream over there is where you get fresh water."

18 "Why didn't you put my camp closer to the stream?"

Skill: Setting

Edwin is setting up Cole's camp near the stream, and trying to give Cole advice about how to function in the wild.

Edwin seems to be humble. His experiences in this setting have shaped him and he has gained wisdom. It seems like he hopes the same for Cole.

19 "Other animals come here for water, too," Edwin said. "How would you feel if a bear made its den beside the stream?"

20 Cole shrugged. "I'd kill it."

21 The potbellied[3] elder nodded with a knowing smile. "Animals feel the same way. Don't forget that." He turned to Cole and placed a hand on his shoulder. Cole tried to pull away, but Edwin gripped him like a clamp. "You aren't the only creature here. You're part of a much bigger circle. Learn your place or you'll have a rough time."

22 "What is there to learn?"

23 "Patience, gentleness, strength, honesty," Edwin said. He looked up into the trees. "Animals can teach us more about ourselves than any teacher." He stared away toward the south. "Off the coast of British Columbia, there is a special black bear called the Spirit Bear. It's pure white and has pride, dignity, and honor. More than most people."

24 "If I saw a Spirit Bear, I'd kill it," Cole said.

25 Edwin tightened his grip as if in warning. "Whatever you do to the animals, you do to yourself. Remember that."

26 "You're crazy, old man," Cole said, twisting free of Edwin's grip. Edwin continued speaking calmly as if nothing had happened. "Don't eat anything unless you know what it is. Plants, berries, and mushrooms can kill you. There's a book in with the supplies to study if you want to learn what is safe to eat. I suggest you read every word. Life is up to you now. I don't know how it was for you in the big city, but up here you live and die by your actions. We'll be out to check on you in a couple of days. After that, Garvey will head home and I'll drop off supplies every few weeks. Any questions?"

27 Cole smirked. He didn't plan on eating any shrubs or berries. "Why did you bring me out so far?" he asked mockingly. "Were you afraid I'd escape?"

3. **potbellied** having a large stomach

28 Edwin looked out across the bay and drew in a deep breath. "Years ago, I was brought here myself when my spirit got lost. This is a good place to find yourself."

29 "This place sucks!" Cole mumbled.

30 Edwin pulled out a key and turned Cole roughly around to remove his handcuffs. "Anger keeps you lost," he said, as he started back toward the shelter. "You can find yourself here, but only if you search."

31 Rubbing at the raw skin on his wrists, Cole followed.

Excerpted from *Touching Spirit Bear* by Ben Mikaelsen, published by HarperCollins.

First Read

Read "Touching Spirit Bear." Then complete the Think Questions below.

THINK QUESTIONS

1. What, if anything, is Garvey's "angle" in the excerpt from Chapter 1? What is he trying to accomplish in his visits with Cole? Use evidence from the text to support your response.

2. Why does Cole agree to live on a secluded island? What does he hope to do once he arrives on the island? Explain, with reference to the text.

3. In the final passage of the excerpt, Edwin tells Cole, "Whatever you do to the animals, you do to yourself. Remember that." What is the meaning of this statement? Why might it be important for young Cole to remember? Cite textual evidence to support your response.

4. Read the following dictionary entry:

   withdraw
   with·draw

   verb

   1. to remove money from a bank account
   2. to no longer participate in a group activity
   3. to leave or exit
   4. to recall or take back a statement

   Decide which definition best matches the word **withdraw** as it is used in "Touching Spirit Bear." Write that definition of *withdraw* here and indicate which clues found in the text helped you determine the meaning.

5. Describing the Alaskan coastline in paragraph 11, the narrator observes that "distant green-black forests were **shrouded** in gray mist." Using context clues, write your best definition of the word *shrouded* and explain how you figured it out.

Skill: Setting

Use the Checklist to analyze Setting in "Touching Spirit Bear." Refer to the sample student annotations about Setting in the text.

••• CHECKLIST FOR SETTING

In order to identify how the plot of a particular story or drama unfolds in a series of episodes, note the following:

- ✓ key elements in the plot
- ✓ the setting(s) in the story
- ✓ how the plot unfolds in a series of episodes
- ✓ how the setting shapes the plot and the characters

To describe how the plot of a particular story or drama unfolds in a series of episodes, consider the following questions:

- ✓ When and where does this story take place?
- ✓ How does the plot unfold in a series of episodes?
- ✓ How does the setting affect the plot? How does it affect the characters and their responses to events? How does the setting help move the plot to a resolution?

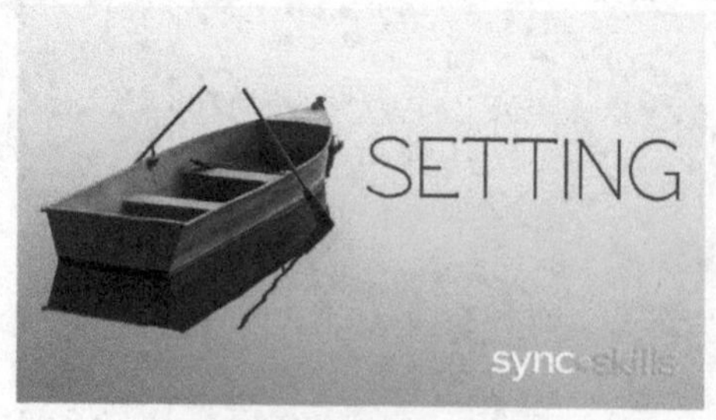

Skill: Setting

Reread paragraphs 23–29 of "Touching Spirit Bear." Then, using the Checklist on the previous page, answer the multiple-choice questions below.

YOUR TURN

1. This question has two parts. First, answer Part A. Then, answer Part B.

Part A: In the excerpt, how does the setting influence Cole's character?

- A. Cole is irritated. He wishes that he could be in another rehabilitation program.
- B. Cole doesn't take Edwin's advice about being one with nature seriously; therefore, Cole is overconfident.
- C. Cole is respectful in his interactions with Edwin as he understands that he must conquer the setting to survive.
- D. Cole does not grasp the idea that he must be one with nature, so he hastily plans an epic escape.

Part B: Which piece of evidence BEST supports your answer to Part A?

- A. "'Patience, gentleness, strength, honesty,' Edwin said."
- B. "'If I saw a Spirit Bear, I'd kill it,'" Cole said.
- C. "'He didn't plan on eating any shrubs or berries.'"
- D. "'This is a good place to find yourself.'"

Close Read

Reread "Touching Spirit Bear." As you reread, complete the Skills Focus questions below. Then use your answers and annotations from the questions to help you complete the Write activity.

SKILLS FOCUS

1. Highlight examples of Cole's responses to his surroundings, to other characters, and to their actions. Explain how Cole's responses influence events in the plot.
2. Identify major events of the plot and summarize what happens in a way that maintains meaning and logical order.
3. Identify evidence of how the setting influences the conflict in "Touching Spirit Bear." Explain the impact of the setting on the conflict.
4. Highlight evidence that indicates the point of view from which the story is told. Identify the point of view and explain why you think the author chose it.
5. Identify evidence that supports the idea that Edwin hopes the island will help Cole become who he is meant to be. Explain your reasoning.

WRITE

NARRATIVE: The excerpt explains that Cole's father "agreed to pay all the expenses of banishment, [as] it was just another one of his buyouts." Pretend that you are Cole's father, and you are writing a letter to your son. Explain your reasons for paying for the Circle Justice program and how you hope it will help Cole change. How do you think this setting will affect Cole's life? Use descriptive details from the text in your letter.

Extended Writing Project

EXTENDED WRITING PROJECT

RESEARCH WRITING

Research Writing Process: Plan

PLAN | DRAFT | REVISE | EDIT AND PUBLISH

Many things you read contain references to people, places, things, and events from different time periods or cultures. *Rosa Parks: My Story*, for instance, takes the reader back in time to the Civil Rights Movement of the 1960s. *Bronx Masquerade* transports readers to a high school in New York City. A reader's curiosity could lead him or her to explore a variety of topics after reading such rich texts.

WRITING PROMPT

Where did Shree Bose draw inspiration for her cancer research? For kids in the 1960s, what were some of the differences between growing up in the North or in the South? Are Spirit Bears real?

Consider the texts included in the *True to Yourself* unit, identify a topic you would like to know more about, and write a research report about that topic. In the process, you will learn how to select a research question, develop a research plan, gather and evaluate source materials, and synthesize and present your research findings. Regardless of which topic you choose, be sure your research paper includes the following:

- an introduction
- supporting details from credible sources
- a clear text structure
- a conclusion
- multimedia components such as charts, images, or video
- a Works Cited page

Writing to Sources

As you gather ideas and information from the texts in the unit, be sure to:

- use evidence from multiple sources; and
- avoid overly relying on one source.

Introduction to Research Writing

Research writing examines a topic and presents ideas by citing and analyzing information from credible, or trustworthy, sources. Good research papers use textual evidence—including facts, statistics, examples, and details from reliable sources—to supply information about a topic and to support analysis of complex ideas. Research helps writers not only discover and confirm facts, but also draw new conclusions about a topic. The characteristics of research writing include:

- an introduction with a clear thesis statement
- supporting details, relevant facts, and quotations from credible sources
- analysis of the details to explain how they support the thesis
- a clear and logical text structure
- parenthetical citations
- a conclusion that wraps up your ideas
- a Works Cited page

As you continue with this Extended Writing Project, you'll receive more instruction and practice at crafting each of the characteristics of research writing to create your own research paper.

Before you get started on your own research paper, read a research paper that one student, Kelaiah, wrote in response to the writing prompt. As you read the Model, highlight and annotate the features of research writing that Kelaiah included in her research paper.

STUDENT MODEL

NOTES

Do Spirit Bears Exist?

1 In *Touching Spirit Bear*, a Tlingit elder named Edwin prepares Cole for living alone on a remote island. He explains, "Off the coast of British Columbia, there is a special black bear called the Spirit Bear. It's pure white, and has pride, dignity, and honor" (Mikaelsen 18). When Cole threatens to kill any Spirit Bear he meets, Edwin warns, "Whatever you do to the animals, you do to yourself" (Mikaelsen 18). Edwin and Cole are fictional characters, but are Spirit Bears real? Spirit Bears do exist. They are considered special not only by the people of the First Nations communities—who have lived near them for thousands of years—but also by researchers and environmentalists. A look at the Spirit Bear's habitat, as well as its cultural and environmental significance, reveals this unique animal's role in the world.

Habitat and Characteristics of Spirit Bears

2 Spirit Bears are a rare subspecies of the American Black Bear. The Spirit Bear is known by different names, including the White Bear, Ghost Bear, Moskgm'ol, Kermode Bear, and its scientific name *Ursus americanus kermodei* (Shoumatoff). The animal lives only in the Great Bear Rainforest, a 21-million-acre wilderness along British Columbia's central coast that has been called "the Amazon of the North" (Kennedy).

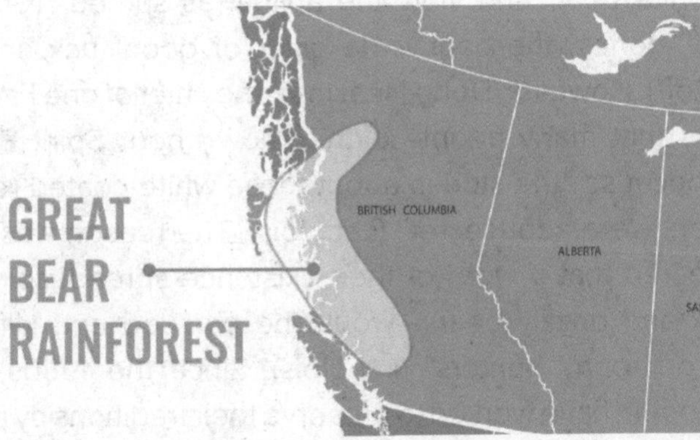

NOTES

3 Unlike the hot, steamy jungles of the Amazon, the Great Bear Rainforest is a cold, rocky island habitat. According to writer Bruce Barcott, the Spirit Bear is "a walking contradiction—a white black bear." Despite having white fur, the Spirit Bear is not a polar bear or an albino. Its cream-colored fur is the result of a rare recessive gene. A white bear cub is produced when both parents, which may be black or white, carry the rare gene (Groc 78–79, Barcott, Shoumatoff).

Spirit Bear Population

4 Only 20 percent of the bears in the Great Bear Rainforest are white (NABC). The bears survive on a diet of salmon, berries, and seaweed (Shoumatoff). There may be as many as 400 or as few as 100 Spirit Bears alive today (Langlois, Groc 79, NABC). As geography professor Chris Darimont explains, "no one really knows how many bears there are in the Great Bear Rainforest" (Shoumatoff). This is because the Spirit Bear has a deep cultural significance to the First Nations people.

Spirit Bears and Indigenous Communities

5 The First Nations communities call the bear "*moskgm'ol*, which means 'white bear,' and view the animal as sacred" (Groc 79). In traditional stories, the bear is "a giver of good luck and power" (Shoumatoff). However, Doug Neasloss, the chief of one First Nations tribe, says that many people didn't know about Spirit Bears until recently because "the stories about these white-coated relatives of black bears were kept secret" (Langlois). The reason was practical: "Elders feared that if word of their existence spread, spirit bears—like black and grizzly bears—would be pursued and killed by fur trappers or trophy hunters" (Langlois). Since the 1980s, the First Nations people have worked to preserve their traditions by protecting

NOTES

the forest and its wildlife. They "believed the forest was worth more intact, and the bears it sheltered—grizzly, black, and Kermode—were worth more to the [First Nations] alive than killed by trophy hunters" (Langlois). Today, people come from all over the world to see the Spirit Bear, not to hunt it.

Protecting Spirit Bears

6 Protecting the Spirit Bear is not just important to the First Nations people; it's also important for the environment. The Spirit Bears play an important role in keeping the rainforest healthy. Spirit Bears take the salmon they catch in the rivers into the forest to eat (Shoumatoff, Groc 79). As the carcasses decay and their nutrients "are absorbed by the forest floor, the nutrients from the ocean are effectively transferred to the trees" (Groc 79). The health of the bears and the forest are connected (Shoumatoff). If the Spirit Bear suffers a decline, so will the rainforest.

Threats to Spirit Bears

7 Today there are many threats to the Spirit Bear, including overfishing, logging, and hunting. Overfishing means there is less food for all the bears in the rainforest. When there are fewer salmon, aggressive grizzlies wander into the Spirit Bears' territory looking for food, and they drive the white bears away (Groc 80, Shoumatoff). In addition, loggers are removing the old cedar trees that Spirit Bears need for hibernating (Groc 82). Hunting is another issue. While it is illegal to kill a Spirit Bear, until 2017 it was legal to hunt black bears, many of which are carriers of the gene needed to produce Spirit Bears (Groc 83, Langlois). Killing a black bear is like killing a Spirit Bear's chances of being born.

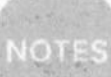

8 In *Touching Spirit Bear*, Cole threatens to kill a Spirit Bear. Edwin reminds him to "learn your place or you'll have a rough time" (Mikaelsen 17). Unlike Cole, the First Nations communities and many scientists and environmentalists recognize the value of the Spirit Bear. While not everyone might believe that the bear has special powers, they, like Edwin, should recognize and respect this animal's important role in the Great Bear Rainforest and its deep connections to the First Nations people.

Works Cited

Barcott, Bruce. "Spirit Bear." *National Geographic,* Aug. 2011, www.nationalgeographic.com/magazine/2011/08/kermode-bear.html.

Groc, Isabelle. "Spirits of the Forest." *BBC Wildlife Magazine,* vol. 33, no. 10, Sept. 2015, pp. 76–83.

Kennedy, Taylor. "Great Bear Rainforest." *NationalGeographic.com,* www.nationalgeographic.com/travel/canada/great-bear-rainforest-british-columbia/.

Langlois, Krista. "First Nations Fight to Protect the Rare Spirit Bear from Hunters." *National Geographic,* 26 Oct. 2017, news.nationalgeographic.com/2017/10/wildlife-watch-hunting-great-bear-rainforest-spirit-bear/.

Mikaelsen, Ben. *Touching Spirit Bear.* HarperCollins Publishers, 2001.

North American Bear Center. "What is a Spirit Bear?" *Bear.org,* 2018, www.bear.org/website/bear-pages/black-bear/basic-bear-facts/101-what-is-a-spirit-bear.html

Shoumatoff, Alex. "This Rare, White Bear May Be the Key to Saving a Canadian Rainforest." *Smithsonian Magazine,* Sept. 2015, www.smithsonianmag.com/science-nature/rare-white-bear-key-saving-canadian-rainforest-180956330/.

WRITE

Writers often take notes about ideas before they sit down to write. Think about what you've learned so far about organizing research writing to help you begin prewriting.

- **Purpose:** What topic from the unit do you find most interesting? What do you want to learn about that topic?
- **Audience:** Who is your audience and what message do you want to express to your audience?
- **Focus:** How can you use a research question to focus your research?
- **Sources:** What kind of sources will help you answer that question?
- **Organization:** What text structure should you use to share the information with readers?

Response Instructions

Use the questions in the bulleted list to write a one-paragraph research summary. Your summary should describe what you plan to research and discuss in your research paper.

Don't worry about including all of the details now; focus only on the most essential and important elements. You will refer back to this short summary as you continue through the steps of the writing process.

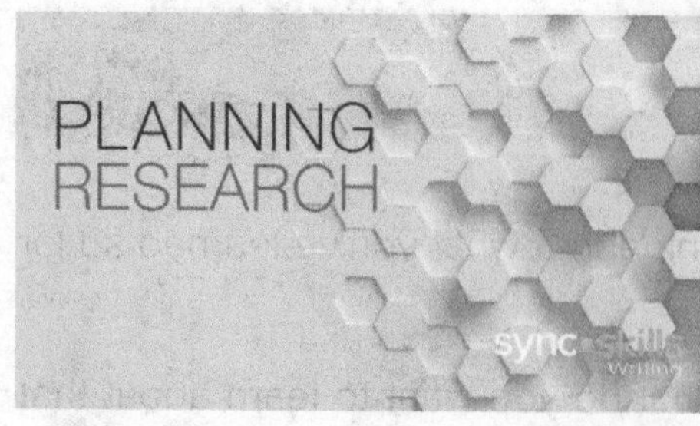

Skill: Planning Research

••• CHECKLIST FOR PLANNING RESEARCH

In order to develop a research plan drawing on several sources, do the following:

- make a list of research tasks
  > if it is not assigned to you, decide on a major research question

  > develop a research plan, a series of steps you can follow to find information to answer your question
- search for information
  > look for information on your topic in a variety of sources, both online and in books and other reference sources

  > if you don't find the information that you need to answer your research question, you may need to modify it

  > refocus and revise your research plan

To develop and revise a research plan, consider the following questions:

- Is the source reliable and credible? How do I know?
- How does the source address themes, concepts, or other areas related to my research?
- Does information in one source contradict, or disprove, information in another source? How might I resolve these differences?
- Do I need to change my major research question?

To write a research plan, follow these steps:

1. Write down the steps you will follow in order to find information that will help you answer your research question. These steps may include looking up your topic in an encyclopedia to gather general information, using online search engines, and checking out books from your school or local library.

2. If you don't find the information you need following your initial research plan, think of other steps you can follow and revise your research plan accordingly.

YOUR TURN

Read the research questions below. Then, complete the chart by matching each question into the correct category.

Research Questions	
A	What sports and teams did Jackie Robinson play for?
B	What kinds of things inspire poets?
C	How did Jackie Robinson succeed?
D	What accomplishments made Eleanor Roosevelt one of the most influential women of her time?
E	How did Jackie Robinson overcome adversity to become a successful baseball player in the all-white league?
F	Why do some First Ladies become famous?
G	Where did Rita Dove draw inspiration for her poetry?
H	Why was Eleanor Roosevelt called *First Lady of the World*?
I	What inspired Rita Dove to write "Rosa"?

Too Narrow	Just Right	Too Broad

 YOUR TURN

Brainstorm questions for formal research. Then evaluate each question to determine whether it is too narrow, too broad, or just right using the secondary set of questions listed in the checklist. Select a question that is just right. Then complete the chart below by writing a short research plan for your report.

Question	Plan
Possible Research Questions:	
Selected Research Question:	
Step 1:	
Step 2:	
Step 3:	
Revise My Research Plan:	

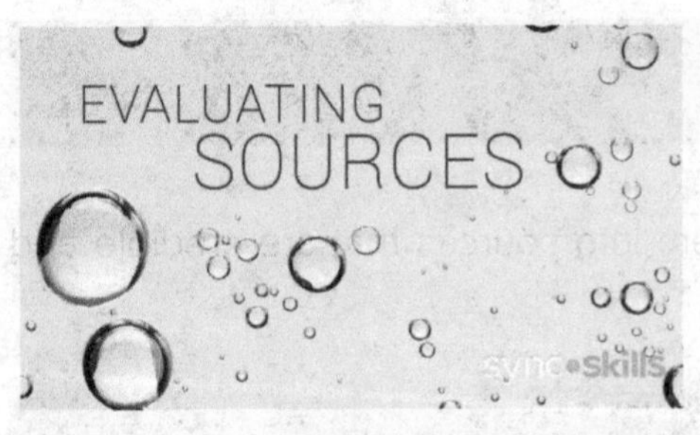

Skill: Evaluating Sources

••• CHECKLIST FOR EVALUATING SOURCES

First, reread the sources you gathered and identify the following:

- what kind of source it is, including video, audio, or text, and where the source comes from
- where information seems inaccurate, biased, or outdated
- where information seems irrelevant or incomplete

In order to use advanced searches to gather relevant, credible, and accurate print and digital sources, use the following questions as a guide:

- Is the source material written by a recognized expert on the topic?
- Is the source material published by a well-respected author or organization?
- Is the material up-to-date or based on the most current information?
- Is the material factual, and can it be verified by another source?
- Is the source material connected to persons or organizations that are objective and unbiased?
- Does the source contain omissions of important information?

After evaluating sources, revise your research plan as needed:

1. Eliminate sources that are not reliable or credible and that contain bias and faulty reasoning.

2. Search for other trustworthy sources that you can use instead.

 YOUR TURN

Read the sentences below. Then, complete the chart by sorting them into sources that are credible and reliable and sources that are not.

Sources	
A	The article has no information about the author other than her name.
B	The author supports arguments with current information and statistics.
C	The text uses clear and strong logic.
D	The author is an environmental scientist.
E	The article leaves out any information that could contradict its main ideas.
F	The text relies on emotional appeals to persuade readers.

Credible and Reliable	Not Credible and Reliable

YOUR TURN

Complete the chart by filling in the title and author of a source and answering the questions about it.

Question	My Source
Source Title and Author	
Reliability: Has the source material been published in a well-established book, periodical, or website?	
Reliability: Is the source material up-to-date or based on the most current information?	
Credibility: Is the source material written by a recognized expert on the topic?	
Credibility: Is the source material published by a well-respected author or organization?	
Bias: Is the source material objective and unbiased?	
Bias: Does the source contain omissions of important information that supports other viewpoints?	
Faulty Reasoning: Does the source contain faulty reasoning?	
Should I use this source in my research report?	

Skill: Research and Note-Taking

••• CHECKLIST FOR RESEARCH AND NOTE-TAKING

In order to conduct short research projects, drawing on several sources and refocusing the inquiry when appropriate, note the following:

- think of a question you would like to have answered
- look up your topic in an encyclopedia to find general information
- find specific, up-to-date information in books and periodicals, on the Internet, and, if appropriate, from interviews with experts
- use the library's computerized catalog to locate books on your topic, and if you need help finding or using any of these resources, ask a librarian
- make sure that each source you use is closely related to your topic
- if necessary, refocus, or change, your topic if you have difficulty finding information about it

To introduce a topic and organize ideas, concepts, and information using an organizational strategy, consider the following questions:

- Is the information relevant and related to my topic?
- Where could I look to find additional information?
- Is the information I have found current and up-to-date?

To synthesize information from sources while taking research notes, follow these steps:

1. Read a source and take notes to gather relevant information about your research topic.
2. Read another source.
3. Identify any new, relevant information that you find in this source.
4. Ask yourself: How does this new information change or refine what I have learned from other sources?
5. Write down notes about how your understanding of your topic has changed or improved through your reading of a variety of sources.

YOUR TURN

Read each bullet point from Kelaiah's note cards below. Then, complete the chart by sorting them into those that are culturally important and those that are environmentally important.

Bullet Points	
A	Source 1: Spirit Bears are important to the Great Bear Rainforest ecosystem and forest growth because they take the salmon they catch back to the forest to eat. As the carcasses decay and their nutrients "are absorbed by the forest floor, the nutrients from the ocean are effectively transferred to the trees" (79).
B	Source 7: Salmon is essential to the ecosystem. Bears carry the salmon into the forest, where the carcasses rot and release nitrogen into the soil. Trees, flowering plants, and even snails and slugs soak up this rich fertilizer. Everything is connected: "the sea feeds the forest, and the bears are the bearers of these nutritious infusions" (Shoumatoff).
C	Source 7: The bear is traditionally seen as "a giver of good luck and power" (Shoumatoff).
D	Source 2: According to First Nations chief Doug Neasloss, until recently many people didn't know Spirit Bears existed because "the stories about these white-coated relatives of black bears were kept secret" (Langlois).
E	Source 1: First Nations communities call the bear "*moskgm'ol,* which simply means 'white bear,' and view the animal as sacred" (79).
F	Source 1: Loggers are removing the old cedar trees that Spirit Bears need for hibernating (82).

Cultural Importance	Environmental Importance

WRITE

Use the steps from the checklist as well as the Skill Model to identify and gather relevant information from a variety of sources. Write note cards for your sources. When you have finished, write a short paragraph that details how you plan to synthesize the information from at least two sources.

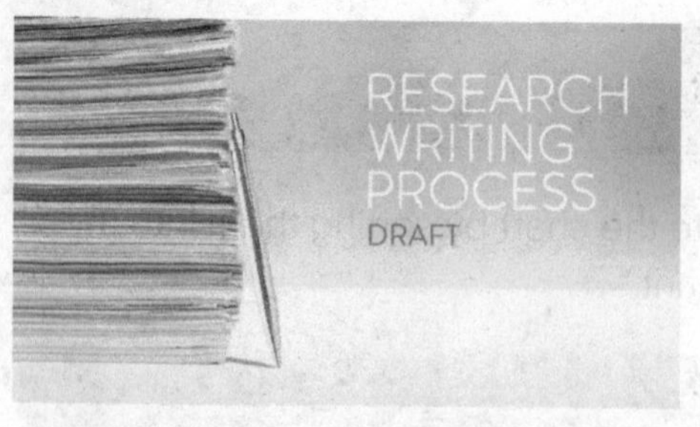

Research Writing Process: Draft

PLAN | DRAFT | REVISE | EDIT AND PUBLISH

You have already made progress toward writing your research paper. Now it is time to draft your research paper.

WRITE

Use your plan, other responses in your Binder, and your source notes to draft your research paper. You may also have new ideas as you begin drafting. Feel free to explore those new ideas as you have them. You can also ask yourself these questions:

- Have I fully supported my thesis statement?
- Have I analyzed information from a variety of sources, including features to gain background information on my topic?
- Have I synthesized information from a variety of sources?
- Have I included supporting evidence from my sources?
- Does the text structure help me to communicate my ideas?

Before you submit your draft, read it over carefully. You want to be sure that you've responded to all aspects of the prompt.

Here is Kelaiah's research paper draft. As you read, identify Kelaiah's main ideas.

STUDENT MODEL: FIRST DRAFT

NOTES

Do Spirit Bears Exist?

In Touching Spirit Bear, Edwin prepares Cole for living alone on a remote island. He explains, Off the coast of British Columbia, there is a special black bear called the Spirit Bear. It's pure white, and has pride, dignity, and honor (Mikaelsen 18). When Cole threatens to kill any Spirit Bear he meets, Edwin warns, "Whatever you do to the animals, you do to yourself (Mikaelsen 18). Edwin and Cole are fictional characters, but are Spirit Bears real? Spirit Bears do exist. They are considered special not only by the people of the first nations communities, who have lived near them for thousands of years, but also by researchers and environmentalists. A look at the Spirit Bear's habitat, as well as its cultural and environmental significance reveals this unique animal's roll in the world.

Spirit Bears are a rare subspecies of the American Black Bear. The Spirit Bear is known by different names, including the White Bear, Ghost Bear, Moksgm'ol, Kermode Bear, and its scientific name Ursus americanus kermodei (Shoumatoff). The animal lives only in the Great Bear Rainforest, which has been called "the Amazon of the North" (Kennedy). Unlike the hot, wet jungles of the Amazon, the Great Bear Rainforest is a cold, rocky island place. According to writer Bruce Barcott, the Spirit Bear is a contradiction. Despite having white fur, the Spirit bear is not a polar bear or an albino. Its cream colored fur is the result of a rare recessive gene (Groc 78, Barcott, Shoumatoff). Only 20 percent of the bears in the Great Bear Rainforest are white (NABC). The bears survive on a diet of salmon, berries, and seaweed (Shoumatoff). There may be as many as 400 or as few as 100 Spirit Bears alive today (Langlois, Groc 79, NABC). As geography professor Chris Darimont explains, no one really knows how many bears there are in the Great Bear Rainforest (Shoumatoff).

NOTES

Skill:
Critiquing Research

Kelaiah used her new note cards as well as information from the sources she had already read to add another section to her informative research paper.

Skill:
Print and Graphic Features

Kelaiah added a heading to be more specific and organized and to better preview the section's content. She also italicized an important word. The image of the Spirit Bear helped convey key ideas to her readers in an interesting way.

Spirit Bears and Indigenous Communities

The First Nations communities call the bear "*moskgm'ol*, which means 'white bear,' and view the animal as sacred" (Groc 79). In traditional stories, the bear is "a giver of good luck and power" (Shoumatoff). However, Doug Neasloss, the chief of one First Nations tribe, says that many people didn't know about Spirit Bears until recently because "the stories about these white-coated relatives of black bears were kept secret" (Langlois). The reason was practical: "Elders feared that if word of their existence spread, spirit bears—like black and grizzly bears—would be pursued and killed by fur trappers or trophy hunters" (Langlois). Since the 1980s, the First Nations people have worked to preserve their traditions by protecting the forest and its wildlife. They "believed the forest was worth more intact, and the bears it sheltered—grizzly, black, and Kermode—were worth more to the [First Nations] alive than killed by trophy hunters" (Langlois). Today, people come from all over the world to see the Spirit Bear, not to hunt it.

~~Protecting the Spirit Bear is not just important to the First Nations people; it's also important for the environment. The Spirit Bears play an important role in keeping the rainforest healthy. Spirit Bears take the salmon they catch in the rivers into the forest to eat (shoumatoff, Groc). As the carcasses decay, their nutrients are absorbed by the forest floor, the nutrients from the ocean are effectively transferred to the trees (Groc). The health of the bears and the forest, are connected (Shoumatoff). If the Spirit Bear suffers a decline, so will the rainforest.~~

Protecting the Spirit Bear is not just important to the First Nations people; it's also important for the environment. The Spirit Bears play an important role in keeping the rainforest healthy. Spirit Bears take the salmon they catch in the rivers into the forest to eat (Shoumatoff, Groc 79). As the carcasses decay and their nutrients "are absorbed by the forest floor, the nutrients from the ocean are effectively transferred to the trees" (Groc 79). The health of the bears and the forest are connected (Shoumatoff). If the Spirit Bear suffers a decline, so will the rainforest.

Skill: Paraphrasing

Kelaiah realized she had plagiarized from "Spirits of the Forest" by Isabelle Groc. She reviewed her notes and the original article to see how she could paraphrase. After highlighting keywords and phrases, Kelaiah also decided to include a quote from the author.

Today there are many threats to the Spirit Bear, including overfishing logging and hunting. Overfishing means there is less food for all the bears in the rainforest. When there are fewer salmon, agresive grizzlies encroach on the Spirit Bears' territory looking for food, and they drive the white bears away (Groc 80, Shoumatoff). In addition, loggers are removing the old cedar trees that Spirit Bears need for hibernating (Groc 82). Hunting is yet another issue. While it is illegal to kill a Spirit Bear, until 2017 it was legal to hunt black bears, many of which are carriers of the gene needed to produce Spirit Bears (Groc 83, Langlois). Killing a black bear is like killing a Spirit Bear's chances of being born.

In Touching Spirit Bear, Cole threatens to kill a Spirit Bear. Edwin reminds him to Learn your place or you'll have a rough time (Mikaelsen 18). Unlike Cole, the first nations communities, and many scientists, and environmentalists recognize the value of the Spirit Bear. While not everyone might believe that the bear has special powers, they, like Edwin, should recognize and respect this animal's important roll in the Great Bear Rainforest and its deep connections to the first Nations people.

Skill: Sources and Citations

Kelaiah adds the website address to the end of the Barcott citation. She adds the publication date to the Groc citation, and she adds the webpage name to the Langlois citation. By including all the required information, Kelaiah gives proper credit to the sources she used. It also lets her readers find these sources.

Works Cited

~~Barcott, Bruce. "Spirit Bear." *National Geographic*, Aug. 2011.~~

~~Groc, Isabelle. "Spirits of the Forest." *BBC Wildlife Magazine*, vol. 33, no. 10, pp. 76–83.~~

Barcott, Bruce. "Spirit Bear." *National Geographic*, Aug. 2011, www.nationalgeographic.com/magazine/2011/08/kermode-bear.html.

Groc, Isabelle. "Spirits of the Forest." *BBC Wildlife Magazine*, vol. 33, no. 10, Sept. 2015, pp. 76– 83.

Kennedy, Taylor. "Great Bear Rainforest." *NationalGeographic.com*, https://www.nationalgeographic.com/travel/canada/great-bear-rainforest-british-columbia/.

~~Langlois, Krista. "First Nations Fight to Protect the Rare Spirit Bear from Hunters." 26 Oct. 2017, https://news.nationalgeographic.com/2017/10/wildlife-watch-hunting-great-bear-rainforest-spirit-bear/.~~

Langlois, Krista. "First Nations Fight to Protect the Rare Spirit Bear from Hunters." *National Geographic*, 26 Oct. 2017, news.nationalgeographic.com/2017/10/wildlife-watch-hunting-great-bear-rainforest-spirit-bear/.

Mikaelsen, Ben. *Touching Spirit Bear.* HarperCollins Publishers, 2001.

North American Bear Center. "What is a Spirit Bear?" *Bear.org*, 2018, https://www.bear.org/website/bear-pages/black-bear/basic-bear-facts/101-what-is-a-spirit-bear.html.

Shoumatoff, Alex. "This Rare, White Bear May Be the Key to Saving a Canadian Rainforest." *Smithsonian Magazine*, Sept. 2015, https://www.smithsonianmag.com/science-nature/rare-white-bear-key-saving-canadian-rainforest-180956330/.

Skill: Critiquing Research

••• CHECKLIST FOR CRITIQUING RESEARCH

In order to conduct short research projects to answer a question, drawing on several sources, do the following:

- gather relevant, or important, information from different print and digital sources
- evaluate your research
- if necessary, refocus or change your question
- assess or evaluate your sources and decide whether they are trustworthy

To evaluate and use relevant information while conducting short research projects, consider the following questions:

- Does my research come from multiple print and digital sources?
- Am I able to evaluate my sources and determine which ones are trustworthy?
- Are there specific terms or phrases in my research question that I can use to adjust my search?
- Can I use "and," "or," or "not" to expand or limit my search?
- Can I use quotation marks to search for exact phrases?

 YOUR TURN

Kelaiah's friend Hope shared her research plan with Kelaiah. In the first column, they listed some critiques of Hope's research. Complete the chart by matching Hope's next steps to each critique.

	Next Steps
A	She should make her search terms more specific by using keywords, phrases, and unique terms with quotation marks and terms like "and," "or," and "not."
B	After doing some research and taking notes, she should think about additional, focused research questions about her topic that will help her modify her research plan.
C	Hope should check that the sources are well-known and respected. She should make sure her sources are from experts in their field, university websites, or well-respected publications. When in doubt, she should ask a teacher.
D	Hope should go to a library and ask the librarian to help find her encyclopedias and nonfiction texts to use in her research paper.

Critiques	Next Steps
Kelaiah is unsure about the accuracy, reliability, and credibility of Hope's sources.	
Hope did a general online search for information and got over a million results.	
Hope only has two sources and both of them are online resources.	
Hope has one general research question, and she is not sure if she will have enough information for a complete informative research paper.	

 YOUR TURN

Complete the chart by answering the questions and writing a short summary of what you will do to make changes to your research plan.

Common Questions or Critiques	My Answers and Next Steps
Do you have enough relevant information from a mix of both digital and print sources?	
Did you use search terms effectively when conducting online searches?	
Are your sources and research accurate, reliable, and credible?	
Did you generate additional, focused questions to further and improve your research?	

Skill: Paraphrasing

••• CHECKLIST FOR PARAPHRASING

In order to paraphrase, note the following:

- make sure you understand what the author is saying after reading the text carefully
- words and phrases that are important to include in a paraphrase to maintain the meaning of the text
- any words or expressions that are unfamiliar
- avoid plagiarism by acknowledging all sources for both paraphrased and quoted material

To paraphrase texts, consider the following questions:

- Do I understand the meaning of the text?
- Does my paraphrase of the text maintain its original meaning? Have I missed any key points or details?
- Have I determined the meanings of any words from the text that are unfamiliar to me?
- Have I avoided plagiarism by acknowledging all my sources for both paraphrased and quoted material?

YOUR TURN

Read the original text excerpt about Langston Hughes in the first column. Complete the chart by matching the keywords to the text excerpt by writing them in the second column. Then, in the third column, paraphrase the original text excerpt using the keywords. Remember to cite the author and page number in parentheses. Part of the first row is done for you as an example.

Keywords				
Paris	jobs	Mexico	reflect	west coast
experience	busboy	Columbia	black	café
Busboys and Poets	1924	Hughes	music	culture
Africa	suffering	travel	America	Midwest
Lincoln	Washington, D.C.	laughter	poet	personal

Original Text Excerpt	Keywords	Paraphrased Text
Hughes had had an incredibly varied life before he became the literary lion of Harlem. He was raised in the Midwest, spent time with his estranged father in Mexico, and studied at Columbia and Lincoln University. He held many jobs, most famously as a busboy—an employment that gives the title to the well-known Washington, D.C. literary café, Busboys and Poets. "Why Langston Hughes Still Reigns as a Poet for the Unchampioned," David C. Ward		To paraphrase: Before settling in Harlem, Hughes had many life experiences. He lived in the Midwest and Mexico, and attended Columbia and Lincoln Universities. He was employed many places, most notably as a busboy at the famous café Busboys and Poets in Washington, D.C. (Ward)

Original Text Excerpt	Keywords	Paraphrased Text
Hughes refused to differentiate between his personal experience and the common experience of black America. He wanted to tell the stories of his people in ways that reflected their actual culture, including both their suffering and their love of music, laughter, and language itself. "Langston Hughes," American Academy of Poets		
Leaving Columbia in 1922, Hughes spent the next three years in a succession of menial jobs. But he also traveled abroad. He worked on a freighter down the west coast of Africa and lived for several months in Paris before returning to the United States late in 1924. By this time, he was well known in African American literary circles as a gifted young poet. "Hughes Life and Career," Arnold Rampersad		

WRITE

Choose one or two parts of your research paper where information is still in the author's words without quotations or citations or where you can better paraphrase. Revise those sections using the questions in the checklist. When you have finished revising this section of your research paper, write out your revision as well as the original excerpt underneath.

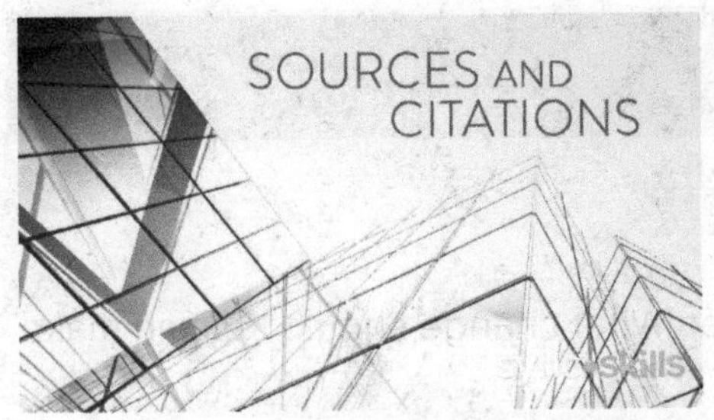

Skill: Sources and Citations

••• CHECKLIST FOR SOURCES AND CITATIONS

In order to cite and gather sources of information, do the following:

- select and gather information from a variety of print and digital sources relevant to a topic
- check that sources are credible, or reliable and trustworthy, and avoid relying on or overusing one source
- be sure that facts, details, and other information support the central idea or claim and demonstrate your understanding of the topic or text
- use parenthetical citations or footnotes or endnotes to credit sources
- include all sources in a bibliography, following a standard format:
  - > Halall, Ahmed. *The Pyramids of Ancient Egypt*. New York: Central Publishing, 2016.
  - > for a citation or footnote, include the author, title, and page number

To check that sources are gathered and cited correctly, consider the following questions:

- Did I give credit to sources for all of my information to avoid plagiarism?
- Have I relied on one source, instead of looking for different points of view on my topic in other sources?
- Did I include all my sources in my bibliography?
- Are my citations formatted correctly using a standard, accepted format?

YOUR TURN

Choose the best answer to each question.

1. Below is a section from a previous draft of Kelaiah's research paper. What change should Kelaiah make to improve the clarity of her citations?

In *Touching Spirit Bear*, Cole threatens to kill a Spirit Bear. Edwin reminds him to "learn your place or you'll have a rough time." Unlike Cole, the First Nations communities and many scientists and environmentalists recognize the value of the Spirit Bear. While not everyone might believe that the bear has special powers, they, like Edwin, should recognize and respect this animal's important role in the Great Bear Rainforest and its deep connections to the First Nations people.

- ○ A. Add the author's last name in parentheses after the quotation.
- ○ B. Add the page number in parentheses after the quotation.
- ○ C. Add the author's last name and the page number in parentheses after the quotation.
- ○ D. No change needs to be made.

2. Below is a section from a previous draft of Kelaiah's Works Cited page. Which revision best corrects her style errors?

The Salmon Bears: Giants of the Great Bear Rainforest. Read, Nicholas, and Ian McAllister. 2010, Orca Book Publishers.

- ○ A. Read, Nicholas, and Ian McAllister. *The Salmon Bears: Giants of the Great Bear Rainforest*. Orca Book Publishers.
- ○ B. *The Salmon Bears: Giants of the Great Bear Rainforest*. Read, Nicholas, and Ian McAllister. 2010, Orca Book Publishers.
- ○ C. Read, Nicholas, and Ian McAllister, 2010. *The Salmon Bears: Giants of the Great Bear Rainforest*. Orca Book Publishers.
- ○ D. Read, Nicholas, and Ian McAllister. *The Salmon Bears: Giants of the Great Bear Rainforest*. Orca Book Publishers, 2010.

WRITE

Use the questions in the checklist to revise your Works Cited list. When you have finished revising your citations, write your list. Refer to the *MLA Handbook* as needed.

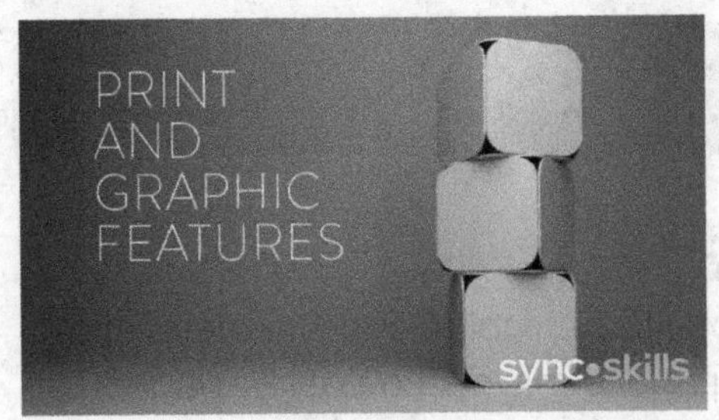

Skill: Print and Graphic Features

••• CHECKLIST FOR PRINT AND GRAPHIC FEATURES

First, reread your draft and ask yourself the following questions:

- To what extent would including formatting, graphics, or multimedia be effective in achieving my purpose?
- Which formatting, graphics, or multimedia seem most important in conveying information to the reader?
- How is the addition of the formatting, graphics, or multimedia useful to aiding comprehension?

To include formatting, graphics, and multimedia, using the following questions as a guide:

- How can I use formatting to better organize information? Consider adding:
  > titles
  > headings
  > subheadings
  > bullets
  > boldface and italicized terms
- How can I use graphics to better convey information? Consider adding:
  > charts
  > graphs
  > tables
  > timelines
  > diagrams
  > figures and statistics
- How can I use multimedia to add interest and variety? Consider adding a combination of:
  > photographs
  > art
  > audio
  > video

 YOUR TURN

Choose the best answer to each question.

1. Kelaiah has decided to include a map image with a body paragraph titled "Habitat and Characteristics of Spirit Bears." Read the section below. How does including a map make this section of her paper more effective?

Habitat and Characteristics of Spirit Bears
Spirit Bears are a rare subspecies of the American Black Bear. The Spirit Bear is known by different names, including the White Bear, Ghost Bear, Moskgm'ol, Kermode Bear, and its scientific name *Ursus americanus kermodei* (Shoumatoff). The animal lives only in the Great Bear Rainforest, a 21-million-acre wilderness along British Columbia's central coast that has been called "the Amazon of the North" (Kennedy).

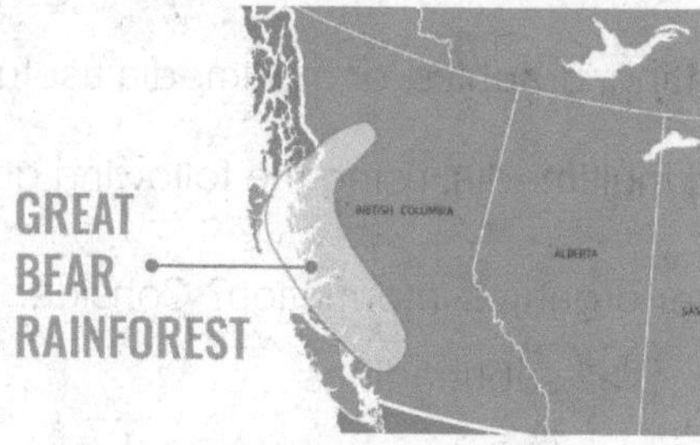

- A. The image helps readers see where Spirit Bears live.
- B. The image helps Kelaiah organize her information more effectively.
- C. The image is an example of multimedia used to add variety and interest to her research paper.
- D. The image is a print feature that will highlight a specific section of the text.

2. Kelaiah needs a heading that best reflects the content of this body paragraph in her draft. Reread the first few sentences of the section and then select the best option.

Only 20 percent of the bears in the Great Bear Rainforest are white (NABC). The bears survive on a diet of salmon, berries, and seaweed (Shoumatoff). There may be as many as 400 or as few as 100 Spirit Bears alive today (Langlois, Groc 79, NABC). As geography professor Chris Darimont explains, "no one really knows how many bears there are in the Great Bear Rainforest" (Shoumatoff). This is because the Spirit Bear has a deep cultural significance to the First Nations people.

- A. Number of Spirit Bears
- B. Spirit Bear Population
- C. Diet of Spirit Bears
- D. Cultural Significance

YOUR TURN

Complete the chart below by brainstorming ideas of how you can use print and graphic features to improve your research paper.

Print and Graphic Feature or Multimedia	My Ideas and Changes
How can I use formatting to better organize information?	
How can I use graphics to better convey information?	
How can I use multimedia to add interest and variety?	

Research Writing Process: Revise

PLAN	DRAFT	REVISE	EDIT AND PUBLISH

You have written a draft of your research paper. You have also received input from your peers about how to improve it. Now you are going to revise your draft.

REVISION GUIDE

Examine your draft to find areas for revision. Keep in mind your purpose and audience as you revise for clarity, development, organization, and style. Use the guide below to help you review:

Review	Revise	Example
	Clarity	
Label details that are important to understanding your topic, such as people, places, or characteristics. Annotate any details where the meaning is unclear.	Add description to clarify the meaning or enhance understanding.	The animal lives only in the Great Bear Rainforest, a 21-million-acre wilderness along British Columbia's central coast that ~~which~~ has been called "the Amazon of the North" (Kennedy).
	Development	
Identify key ideas in your research paper. Annotate places where additional description or information could help develop your ideas.	Make sure you have a strong main idea in each paragraph, and add description or information to develop your ideas.	Despite having white fur, the Spirit Bear is not a polar bear or an albino. Its cream-colored fur is the result of a rare recessive gene. A white bear cub is produced when both parents, which may be black or white, carry the rare gene (Groc 78–79, Barcott, Shoumatoff).

Review	Revise	Example
Organization		
Review your body paragraphs. Identify and annotate any sentences that don't flow in a clear and logical way.	Rewrite the sentences so they appear in a clear and logical order, starting with a strong transition or topic sentence. Make sure to include a transition between body paragraphs.	As geography professor Chris Darimont explains, "no one really knows how many bears there are in the Great Bear Rainforest" (Shoumatoff). This is because the Spirit Bear has a deep cultural significance to the First Nations people. The First Nations communities call the bear "*moskgm'ol*, which means 'white bear' and view the animal as sacred" (Groc 79).
Style: Word Choice		
Identify weak or repetitive words or phrases that do not clearly express your ideas to the reader.	Replace weak and repetitive words and phrases with more descriptive ones that better convey your ideas	Unlike the hot, ~~wet~~ steamy jungles of the Amazon, the Great Bear Rainforest is a cold, rocky island ~~place~~ habitat.
Style: Sentence Variety		
Read your informational essay aloud. Annotate places where introducing quotations from your sources could enhance the academic tone of your paper.	Revise some sentences or paragraphs to include relevant quotations.	According to writer Bruce Barcott, the Spirit Bear is ~~a contradiction.~~ "a walking contradiction—a white black bear."

WRITE

Use the guide above, as well as your peer reviews, to help you evaluate your research paper to determine areas that should be revised. Also be sure to assess how well your print features, graphics, images, videos, or other media help to communicate and support your ideas.

Research Writing Process: Edit and Publish

PLAN | DRAFT | REVISE | EDIT AND PUBLISH

You have revised your research paper based on your peer feedback and your own examination.

Now, it is time to edit your research paper. When you revised, you focused on the content of your research paper. You probably critiqued your research, paraphrased, and looked at your sources, citations, and print and graphic features. When you edit, you focus on the mechanics of your research paper, paying close attention to things like grammar and punctuation.

Use the checklist below to guide you as you edit:

- ☐ Have I used quotation marks and italics correctly?
- ☐ Have I used dashes and hyphens correctly?
- ☐ Have I capitalized the names and titles of people correctly?
- ☐ Do I have any sentence fragments or run-on sentences?
- ☐ Have I spelled everything correctly?

Notice some edits Kelaiah has made:

- Italicize a book title.
- Add a quotation mark to a quotation.
- Capitalize the name of a people.
- Add dashes.
- Correct a spelling error.

In ~~Touching Spirit Bear,~~ *Touching Spirit Bear,* Edwin prepares Cole for living alone on a remote island. He explains, "Off the coast of British Columbia, there is a special black bear called the Spirit Bear. It's pure white, and has pride, dignity, and ~~honor~~ honor" (Mikaelsen 18). When Cole threatens to kill any Spirit Bear he meets, Edwin warns, "Whatever you do to the animals, you do to ~~yourself~~ yourself" (Mikaelsen 18). Edwin and Cole are fictional characters, but Spirit Bears do exist. They are considered special not only by the people of the ~~first nations~~ First Nations ~~communities,~~ communities—who have lived near them for thousands of years—but also by researchers and environmentalists. A look at the Spirit Bear's habitat, as well as its cultural and environmental significance, reveals this unique animal's ~~roll~~ role in the world.

WRITE

Use the questions above, as well as your peer reviews, to help you evaluate your research paper to determine areas that need editing. Then edit your research paper to correct those errors.

Finally, read over your research paper one more time, making sure that you have cited all your sources of quoted, paraphrased, or summarized material. Recall that within the body of your paper, you should put the author's last name and page number, if applicable, in parentheses at the end of the sentence that contains borrowed material. In addition, make sure that all sources cited are listed in your Works Cited list at the end of your research paper. It is very important to cite all your sources so that you can avoid plagiarism.

Once you have made all your corrections, you are ready to publish your work. You can distribute your writing to family and friends, present it to your class, hang it on a bulletin board, or post it on your blog. If you publish online, share the link with your family, friends, and classmates.

Middle School Loneliness

FICTION

Introduction

A Hispanic boy is well-liked at his middle school. He is captain of the basketball team. Then his family moves to a new city. He must attend a new school. The problems begin the very first day. How will he make friends? He must find a way.

VOCABULARY

accurate
free from mistakes; correct

enthusiastic
excited and interested in what is going on

isolated
being alone and apart from others

succeeded
achieved a desired result

READ

1 I used to think I had it made. I was the captain of the basketball team and president of the math club.

2 One summer, my dad accepted a job in a different city and we moved. Worry rained down and soaked into my life as I left my best friends. Like me, they spoke Spanish at home, ate the same foods, and loved basketball. I would be among strangers who might not understand my background. My first day in the new school proved my fears were **accurate**.

3 I was the only Hispanic student. The first week of classes was terrible. I was completely **isolated**. No one spoke to me, and no one sat with me at lunch.

4 Then I saw a notice from Coach Wilson about basketball tryouts. I felt at home as I raced up and down the court trying to impress Coach. He wanted me on the team but warned me things might be difficult. The team members were close friends and did not like strangers. I was new. I liked being on a team again, but Coach's words made me feel uncomfortable.

5 The first practice was disappointing, like other experiences at that school. Jeremy was team captain. His best friend, Nathan, was a great player. Jeremy shouted out orders to others but never to me. Finally, Coach blew the whistle and called for a meeting. He described new plays and said Jeremy was

expected to pass the ball to me. I was supposed to make some baskets. I knew Jeremy and Nathan didn't think I could be a valuable team member. But Coach had spoken, and his word was law on the court.

6 I had no friends on the team. One day, Jeremy and Nathan talked about a hard problem in math class. They said that if they didn't pass Friday's test, they would be off the team. I thought about their problem. They treated me badly, but we couldn't lose great players, and I wanted to win the championship game. I offered to help them, and they accepted.

7 We worked together on the court and off. The team started winning, and **enthusiastic** students came to cheer us on. Jeremy's and Nathan's math grades went up like skyrockets. I didn't sit alone at lunch anymore because my teammates sat with me. Going to a new school is not easy, but I coped with the challenges and **succeeded**.

First Read

Read the story. After you read, answer the Think Questions below.

THINK QUESTIONS

1. What is the main character's problem?

2. Who ends up needing the narrator's help?

3. At the end of the story, what has changed in the narrator's life?

4. Use context to confirm the meaning of the word *enthusiastic* as it is used in "Middle School Loneliness." Write your definition of *enthusiastic* here.

5. What is another way to say that a person feels *isolated*?

Skill: Analyzing Expressions

 DEFINE

When you read, you may find English expressions that you do not know. An **expression** is a group of words that communicates an idea. Three types of expressions are idioms, sayings, and figurative language. They can be difficult to understand because the meanings of the words are different from their **literal**, or usual, meanings.

An **idiom** is an expression that is commonly known among a group of people. For example, "It's raining cats and dogs" means it is raining heavily. **Sayings** are short expressions that contain advice or wisdom. For instance, "Don't count your chickens before they hatch" means do not plan on something good happening before it happens. Figurative language is when you describe something by comparing it with something else, either directly (using the words *like* or *as*) or indirectly. None of the expressions are about actual animals.

••• CHECKLIST FOR ANALYZING EXPRESSIONS

To determine the meaning of an expression, remember the following:

✓ If you find a confusing group of words, it may be an expression. The meaning of words in expressions may not be their literal meaning.

- Ask yourself: Is this confusing because the words are new? Or because the words do not make sense together?

✓ Determining the overall meaning may require that you use one or more of the following:

- context clues
- a dictionary or other resource
- teacher or peer support

✓ Highlight important information before and after the expression to look for clues.

 YOUR TURN

Student Instructions: Read the following excerpt from the text. Then, complete the multiple-choice questions below.

From "Middle School Loneliness"

I heard them say if they didn't pass Friday's test, they'd get kicked off the team. I thought seriously about their problem. We couldn't afford to lose great players.

1. **Based on the excerpt, what could happen to get the boys kicked off the team?**
   - O A. They do their best.
   - O B. They are mean to the narrator.
   - O C. They are not great players.
   - O D. They do not pass a test.

2. **If you are "kicked off" a team, what happens?**
   - O A. You become a starting player for the team.
   - O B. You may no longer play for the team.
   - O C. You play a certain position on the team.
   - O D. You get angry at the team members.

3. **In this excerpt, why is the narrator worried?**
   - O A. He does not want good players to leave his team.
   - O B. He thinks that the boys will blame him.
   - O C. He fears that his problem will affect the team.
   - O D. He believes that his friends need money.

4. **If a team can't "afford to lose great players," what does that mean?**
   - O A. The team needs to spend more to pay the players.
   - O B. The players need to work hard to be great.
   - O C. Losing great players would harm the team.
   - O D. Great players are expensive to find and keep.

Skill: Visual and Contextual Support

 DEFINE

Visual support is an image or an object that helps you understand a text. **Contextual support** is a **feature** that helps you understand a text. By using visual and contextual supports, you can develop your vocabulary so you can better understand a variety of texts.

First, preview the text to identify any visual supports. These might include illustrations, graphics, charts, or other objects in a text. Then, identify any contextual supports. Examples of contextual supports are titles, heads, captions, and boldface terms. Write down your **observations**.

Then, write down what those visual and contextual supports tell you about the meaning of the text. Note any new vocabulary that you see in those supports. Ask your peers and your teacher to **confirm** your understanding of the text.

••• CHECKLIST FOR VISUAL AND CONTEXTUAL SUPPORT

To use visual and contextual support to understand texts, do the following:

- ✓ Preview the text. Read the title, headers, and other features. Look at any images and graphics.
- ✓ Write down the visual and contextual supports in the text.
- ✓ Write down what those supports tell you about the text.
- ✓ Note any new vocabulary that you see in those supports.
- ✓ Create an illustration for the reading and write a descriptive caption.
- ✓ Confirm your observations with your peers and teacher.

YOUR TURN

Suppose that your class created visual supports for some of the sports phrases in "Middle School Loneliness." Match the pictures to the phrases they illustrate.

Phrase Options	
A	make some baskets
B	describe new plays
C	shout out orders
D	pass the ball

1.

2.

3.

4.

Visual Support	Phrase

Close Read

 WRITE

NARRATIVE: The narrator's experience at his new school changes by the end of the story. Reread the last paragraph of the text, and look for examples of how his life is different. Then, write a longer version of the paragraph, and include additional details to explain what school is like for him now. Make sure to include specific words and phrases that help readers understand the narrator's middle school experience. Pay attention to irregularly spelled words as you write.

Use the checklist below to guide you as you write.

- ☐ How has the narrator's life changed?
- ☐ What are some important people or places to the narrator?
- ☐ What words can you include to show middle school life?

Use the sentence frames to organize and write your narrative.

We started to work together. On the court, ______________________________

____.

Jeremy's and Nathan's math grades improved. I continued to help ______________________

____.

I didn't sit alone at lunch anymore. Instead, ______________________________.

Going to a new school is not easy, ______________________________.

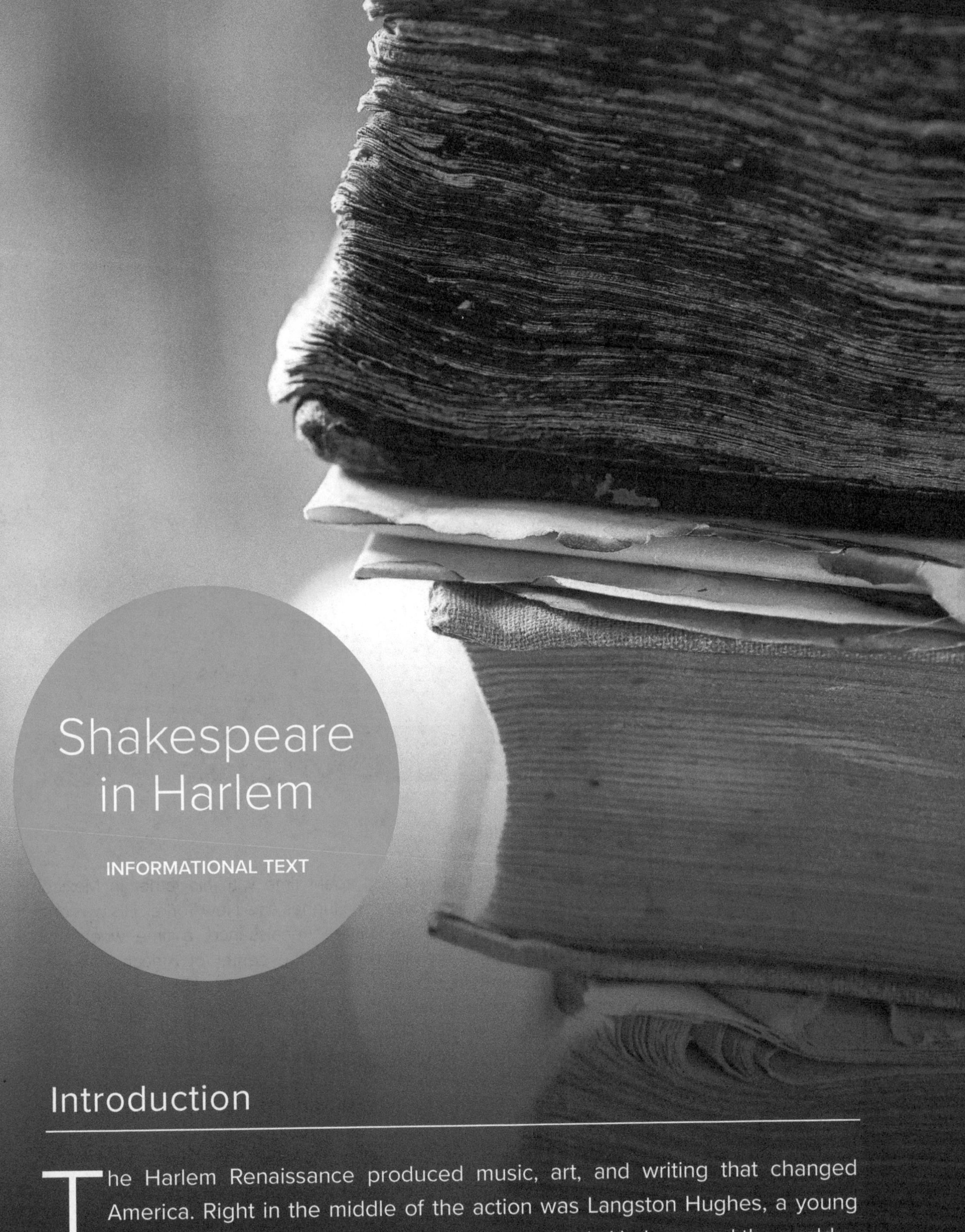

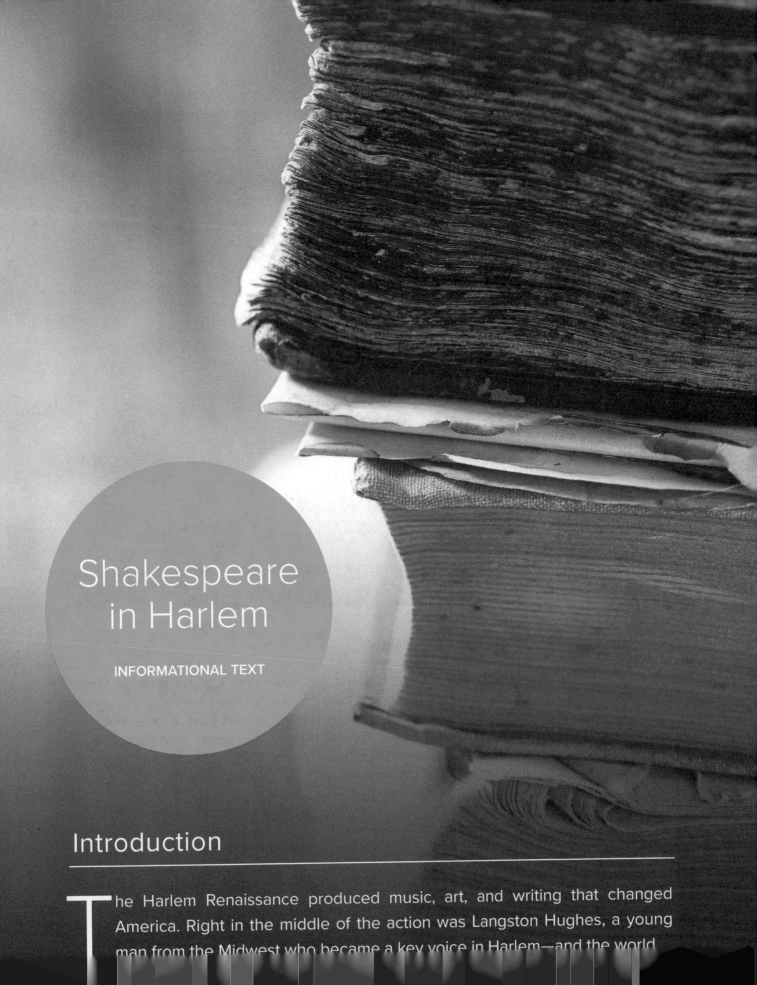

Shakespeare in Harlem

INFORMATIONAL TEXT

Introduction

The Harlem Renaissance produced music, art, and writing that changed America. Right in the middle of the action was Langston Hughes, a young man from the Midwest who became a key voice in Harlem—and the world

VOCABULARY

influenced

had an effect on; guided

deferred

put off to a later time

evokes

recalls to mind

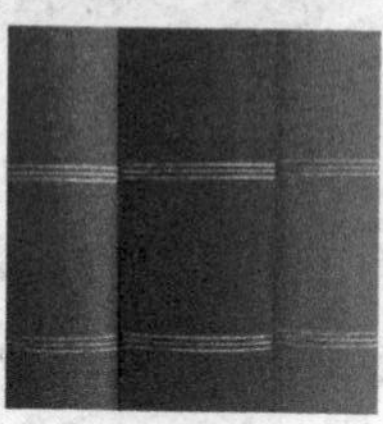

anthologies

published collections of poems or other writings

prolific

very productive

NOTES

READ

1 **Shakespeare in Harlem**

2 He was raised in the Midwest and spent time with his father in Mexico. However, we tend to think of Langston Hughes as a New Yorker. His was one of the strongest voices of the Harlem Renaissance, a time when that neighborhood in New York City became the center of African-American culture. A poet, playwright, novelist, and autobiographer, Hughes earned the nickname "Shakespeare in Harlem."

3 Back in grade school, James Mercer Langston Hughes was already writing. He was named class poet in middle school. His English teachers introduced him to poetry by Carl Sandburg and Walt Whitman. Walt Whitman's poetry had **influenced** Carl Sandburg's work. In turn, both poets influenced Hughes's writing from an early age. His best work **evokes** their interest in ordinary people's everyday lives.

4 Hughes was only 24 when he published his first collection of poetry, *The Weary Blues*. Like much of Hughes's poetry, this book reflects the rhythms and themes of African-American music. This earliest work contains many of Hughes's most famous poems, including "The Negro Speaks of Rivers" and "Dream Variations."

5 Hughes did not just live in Harlem at the liveliest time in its history. He took part in the cultural revolution that was happening there. Drama, painting, music, and writing were part of that revolution. Hughes made friends with many of Harlem's most talented singers, writers, and thinkers.

6 As the Harlem Renaissance ended in the 1930s, Hughes turned his attention to the theater world. Theater was more profitable than poetry. He wrote a play about race in the South. It ran on Broadway for a year. Later, he even wrote words for an opera.

7 By the 1940s, Hughes was writing a newspaper column about racial issues. He continued to write poems. He wrote lyrics for a Broadway musical. He was as **prolific** as Shakespeare. Like Shakespeare, too, he gave us dozens of beautiful lines and phrases that have showed up in other writers' works. Examples include "a raisin in the sun," "a dream **deferred**," "hold fast to dreams," "I am the darker brother," and "black like me."

8 Hughes wrote of the joy and suffering of ordinary people. As he got older, his writing became more political. He protested unfair social conditions. He fought against racism. He tried to give readers pride in their culture. He told his own story in a two-volume autobiography. He won literary prizes. He shared his knowledge with younger writers. Even today, 50 years after his death, his poems continue to appear in **anthologies**. His poem "Harlem" is one of our most popular American poems. Surely, his old nickname was no exaggeration.

First Read

Read the story. After you read, answer the Think Questions below.

THINK QUESTIONS

1. Who is the subject of the biography? Why is he well-known?

2. What was happening in Harlem when Hughes arrived there?

3. What did Hughes write besides poetry?

4. Use context to confirm the meaning of the word *influenced* as it is used in "Shakespeare in Harlem." Write your definition of *influenced* here.

5. What is another way to say that an author is *prolific*?

Skill: Language Structures

 DEFINE

In every language, there are rules that tell how to **structure** sentences. These rules define the correct order of words. In the English language, for example, a **basic** structure for sentences is subject, verb, and object. Some sentences have more **complicated** structures.

You will encounter both basic and complicated **language structures** in the classroom materials you read. Being familiar with language structures will help you better understand the text.

••• CHECKLIST FOR LANGUAGE STRUCTURES

To improve your comprehension of language structures, do the following:

✓ Monitor your understanding.

- Ask yourself: Why do I not understand this sentence? Is it because I do not understand some of the words? Or is it because I do not understand the way the words are ordered in the sentence?

✓ Break down the sentence into its parts.

- Pay attention to comparatives and superlatives. The **comparative** form compares things. The **superlative** form compares more than two things.
- Ask yourself: Are there comparatives or superlatives in this sentence? What are they comparing?
- Form a **comparative** by adding *-er* to the end of the word or by adding *more* before the word.

✓ Confirm your understanding with a peer or teacher.

 YOUR TURN

Read the following excerpt from the text. Then, write the correct adjective to the chart that follows.

> **from "Shakespeare in Harlem"**
>
> Hughes wrote of the joy and suffering of ordinary people. As he got older, his writing became more political. He protested unfair social conditions. He fought against racism. He tried to give readers pride in their culture. He told his own story in a two-volume autobiography. He won literary prizes. He shared his knowledge with younger writers. Even today, 50 years after his death, his poems continue to appear in anthologies. His poem "Harlem" is one of our most popular American poems. Surely, his old nickname was no exaggeration.

Adjectives from the Text	
A	more political
B	younger
C	older
D	most popular

Description	Adjective from the Text
Comparative adjective that compares the age of other writers to Hughes's age	
Superlative adjective that compares one of Hughes's poems to all American poems	
Comparative adjective that compares Hughes's later writing to his earlier writing	
Comparative adjective that compares Hughes's age to his age before	

Skill: Analyzing and Evaluating Text

DEFINE

Analyzing and **evaluating** a text means reading carefully to understand the author's **purpose** and **message**. In informational texts, authors may provide information or opinions on a topic. They may be writing to inform or persuade a reader. In fictional texts, the author may be **communicating** a message or lesson through their story. They may write to entertain, or to teach the reader something about life.

Sometimes authors are clear about their message and purpose. When the message or purpose is not stated directly, readers will need to look closer at the text. Readers can use text evidence to make inferences about what the author is trying to communicate. By analyzing and evaluating the text, you can form your own thoughts and opinions about what you read.

••• CHECKLIST FOR ANALYZING AND EVALUATING TEXT

In order to analyze and evaluate a text, do the following:

✓ Look for details that show *why* the author is writing.

- Ask yourself: Is the author trying to inform, persuade, or entertain? What are the main ideas of this text?

✓ Look for details that show *what* the author is trying to say.

- Ask yourself: What is the author's opinion about this topic? Is there a lesson I can learn from this story?

✓ Form your own thoughts and opinions about the text.

- Ask yourself: Do I agree with the author? Does this message apply to my life?

 YOUR TURN

Read the following excerpt from the text. Then, complete the multiple-choice questions below.

from "Shakespeare in Harlem"

6 By the 1940s, Hughes was writing a newspaper column about racial issues. He continued to write poems. He wrote lyrics for a Broadway musical. He was as prolific as Shakespeare. Like Shakespeare, too, he gave us dozens of beautiful lines and phrases that have showed up in other writers' works. Examples include "a raisin in the sun," "a dream deferred," "hold fast to dreams," "I am the darker brother," and "black like me."

7 Hughes wrote of the joy and suffering of ordinary people. As he got older, his writing became more political. He protested unfair social conditions. He fought against racism. He tried to give readers pride in their culture. He told his own story in a two-volume autobiography. He won literary prizes. He shared his knowledge with younger writers. Even today, 50 years after his death, his poems continue to appear in anthologies. His poem "Harlem" is one of our most popular American poems. Surely, his old nickname was no exaggeration.

1. What is one way in which the author compares Hughes to Shakespeare?

- O A. The author points out that both wrote a great deal.
- O B. The author connects both to a revolutionary time.
- O C. The author demonstrates how their cities shaped them.
- O D. The author suggests that Hughes borrowed words from Shakespeare.

2. What is a second way in which the author compares Hughes to Shakespeare?

- O A. The author indicates that both wrote political tracts.
- O B. The author states that others have used both men's words.
- O C. The author notes that both shared their knowledge with young writers.
- O D. The author suggests that both wrote about ordinary people.

3. What message does the author hope that readers take from this passage?

- O A. A true artist gives readers pride.
- O B. Most poets do other things as well.
- O C. Poets may or may not be remembered.
- O D. Hughes was truly a great talent.

Close Read

 WRITE

LITERARY ANALYSIS: Does the author of "Shakespeare in Harlem" make you believe that Langston Hughes was a great and important writer? Does reading "Shakespeare in Harlem" make you want to read poetry and prose by Langston Hughes? State your feelings about Hughes after having read "Shakespeare in Harlem." Use evidence from the text to support your opinion. Pay attention to possessive case as you write.

Use the checklist below to guide you as you write.

- ☐ How does the author feel about Langston Hughes?
- ☐ What evidence supports that opinion?
- ☐ Is the opinion convincing? Why or why not?
- ☐ What is your reaction to what you read?

Use the sentence frames to organize and write your literary analysis.

The author of "Shakespeare in Harlem" believes that Langston Hughes ______________________________

____.

The author includes evidence such as ______________________ and ______________________.

Based on what I read in "Shakespeare in Harlem," I now think that ______________________________

____.

PHOTO/IMAGE CREDITS:

cover, iStock.com/littleny
Svetlana Chmakova - Vince Talotta / Contributor/ Toronto Star/ Getty Images
Rita Dove - Getty Images Europe: Barbara Zanon / Contributor
W.E.B. DuBois - nsf / Alamy Stock Photo
Russell Freedman - Randy Duchaine / Alamy Stock Photo
Henry Ford - GL Archive / Alamy Stock Photo
Nikki Grimes - Photo credit: Aaron Lemen
Rebecca Harrington - New York Daily News / Contributor/ New York Daily News/ Getty Images
Jackie Robinson - Everett Collection Inc / Alamy Stock Photo
p. 5, iStock.com/littleny
p. 7, iStock.com/
p. 8, iStock.com/littleny
p. 9, iStock.com/ai_yoshi
p. 12, ©iStock.com/RomoloTavani
p. 13, StudySync
p. 14, Shree Bose
p. 15, Shree Bose, Photo by Andrew Federman
p. 17, Official White House Photo by Pete Souza, StudySync
p. 18, StudySync
p. 19, Piper
p. 21, ©iStock.com/RomoloTavani
p. 22, iStock.com/Hohenhaus
p. 23, iStock.com/Hohenhaus
p. 24, iStock.com/janrysavy
p. 25, iStock.com/janrysavy
p. 26, ©iStock.com/RomoloTavani
p. 27, iStock.com/SteffenHoejager
p. 30, iStock.com/SteffenHoejager
p. 31, iStock.com/fotogaby
p. 32, iStock.com/fotogaby
p. 33, iStock.com/donatas1205
p. 34, iStock.com/donatas1205
p. "35, iStock.com/SteffenHoejager
p. 36, iStock.com/ErikaMitchell
p. 40, iStock.com/
p. 42, Underwood Archives/Archive Photos/Getty Images
p. 46, Underwood Archives/Archive Photos/Getty Images
p. 47, iStock.com/eskaylim
p. 48, iStock.com/eskaylim
p. 49, iStock.com/Martin Barraud
p. 50, iStock.com/Martin Barraud
p. 51, iStock.com/Orla
p. 52, iStock.com/Orla
p. 53, Underwood Archives/Archive Photos/Getty Images
p. 54, Public Domain
p. 58, iStock.com/baona
p. 59–72, From Brave by Svetlana Chmakova. Copyright © 2017 by Svetlana Chmakova. Used by permission of Yen Press, an imprint of the Hachette Book Group USA Inc.
p. 73, iStock.com/baona
p. 74, iStock.com/antoni_halim
p. 75, iStock.com/antoni_halim
p. 76, iStock.com/baona
p. 77, iStock.com/PaulTessier
p. 81, iStock.com/PaulTessier
p. 82, iStock.com/Brostock
p. 83, iStock.com/Brostock
p. 84, iStock.com/ThomasVogel
p. 85, iStock.com/ThomasVogel
p. 86, iStock.com/PaulTessier
p. 87, ©iStock.com/sarkophoto
p. 92, ©iStock.com/sarkophoto
p. 93, iStock.com/Max_Xie
p. 94, iStock.com/Max_Xie
p. 95, ©iStock.com/sarkophoto
p. 96, iStock.com/hanibaram, iStock.com/seb_ra, iStock.com/Martin Barraud
p. 97, iStock.com/Martin Barraud
p. 99, StudySync Graphic
p. 100, iStock/jonmccormackphoto
p. 101, Paul Nicklen/National Geographic Image Collection/ Getty Images
p. 104, iStock.com/koya79
p. 107, iStock.com/Mutlu Kurtbas
p. 110, iStock.com/DNY59
p. 112, iStock.com/Martin Barraud
p. 114, Paul Nicklen/National Geographic Image Collection/ Getty Images
p. 117, iStock.com/SKrow
p. 120, iStock.com/horiyan
p. 123, iStock.com/tofumax
p. 125, iStock.com/me4o
p. 128, iStock.com/Martin Barraud
p. 130, iStock.com/Martin Barraud
p. 132, iStock.com/sharpshutter
p. 133, iStock.com/Kerkez
p. 133, stevecoleimages/iStock
p. 133, iStock.com/Jewelsy
p. 133, petesaloutos/iStock
p. 135, iStock.com/sharpshutter
p. 136, iStock.com/Ales_Utovko
p. 138, iStock.com/AlexandrBognat
p. 139, iStock.com/RapidEye
p. 139, iStock.com/slobo
p. 139, iStock.com/Wavebreakmedia
p. 139, iStock.com/Rawpixel
p. 140, iStock.com/sharpshutter
p. 141, iStock.com/
p. 142, iStock/mangostock
p. 142, iStock.com/Giulio_Fornasar
p. 142, iStock.com/hanohiki
p. 142, iStock.com/
p. 142, iStock.com/
p. 144, iStock.com/
p. 145, iStock.com/BlackJack3D
p. 147, iStock.com/kyoshino
p. 149, iStock.com/

studysync

Text Fulfillment Through StudySync

If you are interested in specific titles, please fill out the form below and we will check availability through our partners.

ORDER DETAILS

Date:

TITLE	AUTHOR	Paperback/ Hardcover	Specific Edition *If Applicable*	Quantity

SHIPPING INFORMATION

Contact:

Title:

School/District:

Address Line 1:

Address Line 2:

Zip or Postal Code:

Phone:

Mobile:

Email:

BILLING INFORMATION

☐ *SAME AS SHIPPING*

Contact:

Title:

School/District:

Address Line 1:

Address Line 2:

Zip or Postal Code:

Phone:

Mobile:

Email:

PAYMENT INFORMATION

☐ CREDIT CARD

Name on Card:

Card Number: Expiration Date: Security Code:

☐ PO

Purchase Order Number:

StudySync Text Fulfillment, BookheadEd Learning, LLC
610 Daniel Young Drive | Sonoma, CA 95476